ZEN MIRACLES

Zen Miracles

Finding Peace in an Insane World

Brenda Shoshanna, Ph.D.

John Wiley & Sons, Inc.

Published by John Wiley & Sons, Inc., New York
Published simultaneously in Canada

The author and publisher gratefully acknowledge the following sources for their permission to include copyrighted material: from *The Kabir Book* by Robert Bly, © 1971, 1977 by Robert Bly, © 1977 by the Seventies Press, reprinted with permission of Beacon Press, Boston; from *Tao of Zen* by Ray Grigg, reprinted with permission of Charles E. Tuttle Co., Boston, Mass. and Tokyo, Japan; from *Call Me By My True Names: The Collected Poems of Thich Nhat Hanh* by Thich Nhat Hanh, reprinted with permission of Parallax Press, Berkeley, Calif. © 1999; from *The Three Pillars of Zen* by Roshi Philip Kaplean, reprinted with permission of Doubleday, a division of Random House; from *Zen Flesh, Zen Bones* by Paul Reps and Nyogen Senzaki, © 1994 by Paul Reps and Nyogen Senzaki, reprinted by arrangement with Shambhala Publications, Inc., Boston, www.shambhala.com; from *Delicious Laughter* by Jelaluddin Rumi, reprinted with permission of Maypop Books © 1990; from *Two Zen Classics* by Katsuki Sekida, reprinted with permission of Weatherhill Publishers © 1977.

This publication is designed to provide accurate and authoritative information in regard to the subject matter covered. It is sold with the understanding that the publisher is not engaged in rendering professional services. If professional advice or other expert assistance is required, the services of a competent professional person should be sought.

Library of Congress Cataloging-in-Publication Data:
Shoshanna, Brenda.
    Zen miracles : finding peace in an insane world / Brenda Shoshanna.
        p. cm.
    Includes bibliographical references and index.
    ISBN 0-471-41481-6
        1. Peace of mind—Religious aspects—Zen Buddhism. 2. Meditation—Zen Buddhism. I. Title.

BQ9265.4 .S48 2002
294.3'444—dc21   2001046958

Printed in the United States of America
10 9 8 7 6 5 4 3 2 1

This book is dedicated to the Infinite One whose great miracle allowed me to meet this teaching, to practice, and to make an offering of what I have begun to learn.

Acknowledge Him in all your ways,
And He will direct the steps of your feet.

—*the Torah*

Contents

PART FOUR

DISSOLVING THE FALSE SELF

PART FIVE

ZEN, GOD, AND ENLIGHTENMENT

ACKNOWLEDGMENTS

To the lively, courageous spirit of my original teachers, Soen Nakagawa Roshi and Eido Roshi, and to my grandfather, Reb Moshe Yitzchak Snitofsky, who loved God so much his entire life turned into a song.

SPECIAL THANKS

First and foremost let me acknowledge my outstanding agent, Noah Lukeman, without whose continuous support, effort, and inspiration this book would never have been written. I also wish to especially thank my fine editor, Tom Miller, whose enthusiasm, guidance, and excellent direction helped make the book what it is.

Without the tireless efforts of my teachers, I would never have been able to put these words on paper, or to have the smallest taste of practice. I wish to acknowledge and thank my teachers, Soen Roshi, Eido Roshi, and Joko Charlotte Beck, without whom my practice would never be what it is.

Many beautiful dharma friends have guided, encouraged, and deeply inspired me, and continue to do so—first, with particular thanks for their outstanding support, Jeffrey Azbell, Daniel Myerson, Carolyn Stark, Fran Perillo, Fay Tabakman, and William Solomon. I also thank Yoshi Amakawa, Kuju, Sara Birnbaum, Seppo, Ed Ferrey, Peter Gamby, Chinshu Scott Young, Wado, Vicky Gerdy, Bompo, Haskell Fleishaker, Yayoi, Karen Matsumoto, Katsuro, Anthony McKiernen, Kushu, Master Min Pai, Kanzan, Bruce Rickenbacker, Dogo, Don Scanlon, Enyo, Carolyn Stark, Kyoshin, and Jacques Van Engel.

With loving appreciation I also offer deep thanks for the wisdom and inspiration received from Rabbi Ephraim Wolf and the Lubovitcher Rebbe. For all of this I am immensely grateful.

Last, but not least of all, without my wonderful family and their continual love, it would have been impossible to even dream of embarking upon such a project. Great thanks to all of them, Gerry, Leah, Melissa and Abram, Joshua and Yana, Adam, Taisan, Zoe, Remy, and the amazing Jacob Benjamin.

ZEN
MIRACLES

INTRODUCTION

> A young shoot has borne
> Beautiful flowers
> Growing upon an aged plum tree
> —*Basho*

We all want life to be miraculous, and it is. We pray for miracles, seek miracles, listen to stories about miracles, and think miracles will happen someday in the future, or happened thousands of years ago. So few realize that the great miracle is happening in our lives, right now. Zen is simply the practice of waking up so we can see the miracle, give thanks, and live with it wholeheartedly.

The practice of Zen has befuddled and fascinated people throughout time. A true description of what it is cannot be given in words. In Zen, we say as soon as you speak, you are far from the mark. According to an ancient Zen saying, "Wash out your mouth before you speak about Zen." Words limit, cheapen, and distort understanding. And yet, remaining silent will not do, either. This itself is a *koan*—a Zen riddle—or challenge for us.

Zen descends from a monastic tradition. It has traveled through many nations and cultures, and now is being brought to this country, where it is greatly needed. We must learn to integrate it, along with its ancient traditions, into our culture and our everyday lives.

I was raised in a Hasidic Jewish environment, in Borough Park, Brooklyn, yet in a family where each person strongly held a different point of view. I was fascinated by koans (which I'll explain later) right from the start, though I did not call them that. A longing for God, mixed with confusion, conflict, and divided loyalties besieged me. Then, one day, at the age of fifteen, hav-

1

ing been ripped out of Yeshiva and now attending public high school, a strange thing happened. A history teacher came over and gave me a gift wrapped in a brown paper bag.

"Don't tell anyone about this," he said secretively. "It's perfect for you and I know it." I had no idea what it was.

I went home and undid the package. Inside was a book by D. T. Suzuki on Zen. I opened the pages, began to read, and was filled with inexplicable joy. I read one koan after another, had no idea what they meant, but knew that this could finally lead me to exactly what I'd been yearning for.

I held on to that book for many years, taking it wherever I went, and reading it over and over again. When friends asked what it meant, I couldn't say. I only felt strongly that this was a passageway to the truth.

For many years I did not realize that there was a specific "practice" of Zen. I also had no idea where I would ever find a teacher. At times I would ask friends if they thought I would have to go to Japan to find a teacher. A particularly kind and wise friend, Gerry, used to tell me, "Nope, I think he'll just arrive one day by himself."

About seventeen years after that, it happened. I found a teacher, a place to practice, and was instructed in *zazen*, or sitting meditation. Day by day, a whole new life opened up, including powerful memories and longings of childhood. Sitting on the cushion was not an escape from anything, nor was it, for me, the acceptance of a new "religion." It was practice, practice, practice. It made me tackle all parts of my life, including my own connection to God and my heritage, which grew deeper and more vivid each day as I sat. It also forced me to look differently at my psychological practice, my patients, marriage, children—every part of my life.

Conventional wisdom has a saying, "You cannot return home again." Zen practice disagrees. "Each time we sit, we return home." Eventually, some of us may also have to actually return to the streets and the background we came from, bringing along what we found.

Zen Miracles is an attempt to digest my experience as a Westerner, a practicing psychologist, a therapist, a mother, and a householder with Zen, and to offer whatever I may have learned to whomever it may be helpful.

Having worked as a psychologist and therapist for over twenty-five years, it has become clearer and clearer to me that no matter how many problems are worked through, true peace and fulfillment may still be elusive. Once one issue is resolved, another arises to take its place. Particularly today, as we seek more and more success, money, skills, and possessions, the great miracle of life itself goes undetected. Many live their precious days feeling like beggars and losers, bringing resentment to the great feast of life. This book is dedicated to our being able to become aware of the gifts and miracles we receive daily. It focuses on understanding and removing the veils that cloud us, the inner and outer hindrances that turn friends into enemies, joy into suffering, and heaven itself into hell. This is not the fault of anything outside ourselves. It is simply the nature of the deluded mind.

Until the deluded mind is recognized for what it is and is weakened, we are not able to know who we are and where we are going, or to appreciate the great miracle of life.

Zen Miracles shows specifically how Zen practice approaches the deluded mind and the problems, struggles, and relationships we are faced with day by day. Written by a psychologist and long-term Zen practitioner, the book contrasts our usual ways of working out problems with the way of Zen. Rather than seeking to diagnose illness, prescribing medication to numb the pain, correcting deficiencies, or seeing ourselves as weak or sinning, Zen takes another tack. It points to our fundamental strength and beauty—our "Buddha Nature"—and spends time strengthening that. As we do this, depression, conflict, and other disturbances fall away by themselves.

Ultimately, the reader will discover that Zen practice is not exotic and difficult, but an amazingly simple and powerful way to enhance one's everyday life. Whatever presents itself to us is not rejected, but becomes our practice. We do not judge or condemn anything, just seek to understand the essential nature of experience itself.

Also, unlike psychological work, we do not spend time pruning the branches of a tree (solving one problem only to find another), but go deeper and pull out the actual root. We go to the root of our suffering and deal with it directly.

When we approach life in this manner, stress, confusion, loneliness, anger, and many other forms of distress dissolve right before our eyes. The calmness, compassion, and clarity generated by this practice have never been more deeply needed. There is no better medicine.

Zen Miracles is divided into five parts: 1) Getting Started—the specifics of practice, how to do it, what it entails; 2) Cravings and Compulsions—a look at our psychological nature from the Zen point of view, including the three poisons and the effects of karma upon our lives; 3) Letting Go—the essence of letting go, forgiving, and dissolving obstacles in our lives; 4) Dissolving the False Self—new look at our sense of identity and the ways in which false ego distorts, constricts, and causes great pain; and 5) Zen, God, and Enlightenment—integrating Zen practice into the Judeo-Christian world with a look at precepts, commandments, cautions, and life values, which accompany healthy practice.

Because the emphasis in *Zen Miracles* is always upon integrating practice with family, work, relationships, and everyday life, the book includes exercises that can be done wherever one is, and help to make the Zen principles our own.

Along with zazen, it is of crucial importance to take this practice into all the activities we find ourselves in. Exercises are offered in each chapter to allow the reader do this. These exercises, called Zen in Action, prepare us for other forms that practice takes, such as cleaning, cooking, eating, sleeping, walking, laughing, koan study, *sesshin* (retreats), and *dokusan* (interviews with the master).

The reader will have a sense of Zen history as he or she hears the questions, answers, shouts, anecdotes, and life experiences of some great teachers of the past. They will also hear of the experiences of present-day Zen students, and the way the practice has borne fruits in their lives.

Zen Miracles is a practical book, geared toward offering the reader an entrée into this ancient world, making it accessible without losing the authenticity and dynamism that it can bring. Even a few moments of practice, done fully, can alter the rest of the day. This practice proceeds breath by breath, moment by moment—it is never too early, or too late.

> Zazen is not a difficult task, just free yourself from all incoming complications and hold your mind against them like a great iron wall. Then someday you will meet your true Self as if you had awakened from a dream, and will have the happiness you never could have derived otherwise.
>
> —*Soyen Shaku*

PART ONE

GETTING STARTED

CHAPTER 1

What Is Zen?

ZEN MIRACLE 1
*You can laugh when you laugh
and cry when you cry.*

An ancient Zen story tells that centuries ago, a physician, faced daily with death and suffering, sought out the guidance of a famous Zen Master who was living quietly in an inaccessible mountain hut. The physician climbed the mountain, searched for the hut, and, after many days, found him raking leaves at the side of his tiny house. The teacher did not look up when the student arrived, but kept raking slowly.

> "I have come to understand the essence of Zen," the physician proclaimed. The Zen Master looked up for a moment. "Go home and be kind to your patients," the Master replied. "That is Zen."
>
> —*Ancient Zen story*

FINDING YOUR ANSWERS

Most questions have answers. They are addressed to our rational mind. We want information we can get our hands around, answers to quench our insatiable thirst to know and do what's right, to handle the unending complications life presents. We strategize, plan, and gather whatever facts we can find. We search for authorities, assuming someone out there has our answer. This search can become a mania, as we run to teachers, doctors, psychologists, priests, and rabbis in the belief they have the "right way." Wars have been fought and lives have been sacrificed in the effort to protect the right answer or system.

The answers to Zen questions cannot be found by thinking, talking, or finding a Zen Master or other authority. A Zen Master can only prod, kick, yell, cajole, love, and shove you into realizing that no one else has your truth. To find the answers to your life questions, you must look within. Nothing less will do. Nothing more is needed.

Zen is about finding and honoring the head on your own shoulders, the heart that's beating right now inside of you. It's about turning the search around, discovering and trusting what's within.

> Don't put a head on your own head. What's wrong with the one you have?
>
> —*Nyogen Senzaki*

Don't Put a Head on Your Own Head

Zen practice is authoritarian and antiauthoritarian at the same time. It is antiauthoritarian in the sense that Zen students are taught how to totally reclaim their lives and their minds. They become able to take back all the scattered power and energy they have given to the thousands of "authorities" they have found or projected in the outside world. After years of practice, a Zen student is finally able to walk on this earth with his own two feet, to live the life given to him. He is able to laugh when he laughs, cry when he cries. He is wholehearted and without deception.

Eat When You're Hungry, Sleep When You're Tired

Rinzai Gigen was the founder of one of the main schools of Zen. He died in A.D. 866; the date of his birth is unknown. Rinzai Zen is known for its dynamism and uncompromising directness. His teaching was brought to Japan in the thirteenth century.

Rinzai said, "When I'm hungry, I eat, when I'm tired I sleep. Fools laugh at me. But the wise understand." *(Rinzai Roku)*

How many of us can really eat when we're hungry, or sleep when tired? For many it is difficult to even recognize hunger for what it is. When we're hungry we talk, search for love, diet, or gobble down the wrong food. When we're tired we push ourselves to work harder, run, dance, or fall into bed and toss all night with difficult dreams. How many of us can really taste the food we are eating, appreciate it, and digest it? How many of us know sleep that truly refreshes, innocent sleep like that of a little child?

Laura's Story

Laura, a mother in her mid-forties who had always led a life of good health, woke up one day to find herself feeling ill. She initially discounted it for a passing virus, but weeks passed and it remained. Her moods became uncontrollable, and finally her balance was off and her eyes were swollen. After visiting a number of doctors, she was finally diagnosed with a thyroid disorder. Laura was put on medication and was told she may or may not get better. Months passed, but with no improvement. Desperate, she tried acupuncture, herbs, and a host of other alternative remedies, and yet her condition remained unchanged.

One afternoon a friend offered to teach her Zen meditation. Laura felt she had nothing to lose. She followed the basic instructions, spending about an hour that day with her friend. "It felt good," Laura said, "but not spectacular. Bells didn't go off. I didn't get high." Nevertheless, something drew her back to the meditation cushion, and she decided, from that point on, to spend an hour a day sitting on her own.

Within six months of steady Zen practice, Laura's eyes became normal, her moods steadied, she became balanced again. Now, when asked about Zen, she says, "I don't know exactly what happened, but it has simply saved my life."

What Is the Illness?

The whole world is medicine
What is the illness?
—*Ancient Zen saying*

What exactly is the illness that Laura was suffering from? Most come to the *zendo* (the meditation place) to practice because they are suffering with many problems, anxiety, dissatisfaction in life. Something is wrong—missing. No matter what other paths they've chosen, this churning inside goes on and on.

Buddha described this churning beautifully. When asked who he was, he said, "I'm a doctor who's come to cure the ills of the world. We've all been shot by a poison arrow and I will show you how to pull the arrow out." He never said, "I'm going to pull it out for you." In Zen practice we do not depend on others, but instead learn how to pull our own poison arrows out.

Most of us spend our time discussing and analyzing the nature of our suffering, figuring out who can help. Here, in Zen practice, we put an end to discussion, and just take the arrow and pull it out. After the arrow is removed, people are often amazed to discover that many of the things they longed for, chased after, and thought they couldn't live without, were the poison itself.

WHAT IS ZEN? 13

My Eyebrows Are Horizontal — My Nose Is Vertical

After years of practice, when Dogen Zenji (a great, ancient teacher of Zen) returned to Japan he was asked what he learned there.

"I learned that my eyebrows are horizontal and my nose is vertical," he said.

The questioner looked at him, amazed. "Everyone knows that."

But the questioner was wrong. How long does it take for us to see things exactly as they are? How many of us can tolerate that? The basic truth of the matter is:

> Humankind cannot bear very much reality.
>
> —*T. S. Eliot*

Because we cannot bear very much reality we often escape to illusions to soothe us, a process that can cause enormous disappointment and pain. However, reality *is* the medicine. The facts of our lives, when we are able to know them, will free us from the torment we are in. When we can bear reality thoroughly, suffering is over. Pain may exist, but it is only pain. Suffering is what we add to pain. It is the refusal to experience life as it is, moment by moment. It is the many layers of fabrications—meanings and interpretations—we add to whatever we come up against.

After facing an illness, difficulty, or other catastrophe, a craving comes to understand. Some think, *This would never have happened if I were a better person.* Or, *Someone else is to blame for my suffering.* Or, *The meaning of this event is that I'm bad, I'm hated, my suffering will eradicate all my sins.*

We can imagine all kinds of explanations, but the deepest truth is, we don't know. Explanations bring superficial consolation. A don't-know mind is different. It is able to take life as it is given, and no matter what happens, to dare to get up and live. A don't-know mind is humble and supple. It does not impose itself upon the facts of life. It eliminates catastrophic expectations. It learns to simply accept and go on.

The World of Feelings and Ideas

The interpretations we bring to our experience, the thoughts and meanings we arrive at, are the essence of psychological study. Psychologists analyze the content and origin of our thought processes. Some thoughts or obsessions are viewed as a defense against unacceptable memories or emotions. Other thoughts are traced back to their origin, perhaps as a reaction to a punitive parent. By exploring thoughts, feelings, and interpretations, the patient learns to reframe his or her world, to respond differently. There is nothing intrinsically wrong with this except that both the patient and therapist are spending most of their time in the world of feelings and ideas. By doing so, both may become disconnected from the vital reality presenting itself at that moment. Both may not be able to feel the spring breeze blowing on their faces, or the loving touch of a new friend.

Even when the assumptions of psychology are valid on a certain level of truth, Zen practice responds by saying that all mental machinations are off the mark. They themselves are the cause of suffering, separating us from the direct experience of the plain facts of our lives. All the insight we will ever need to live well will come from fully being who and where we are.

Pain Is Simply Pain

When we let mental machinations go, pain is simply pain. It cannot be avoided in life. To try to avoid it is part of the sickness. The more we are able to experience and accept it, the sooner our suffering subsides. We do not need to explain away pain. We cannot figure it out. We can, however, receive it. In the simple receiving, pain transforms into something quite different. Not only does the pain transform, but more important, *we* do. As we practice Zen we see that pain is not bad. It is simply pain. If we spend our lives running away from painful moments, we shut out a great deal of what life brings us, both the pain and the joy. We can neither laugh when we're happy nor cry when we're sad.

In Zen, we learn how to feel and accept painful moments, to become larger than our pain. When we are willing to accept our experience, just as it is, a strange thing happens: it changes into something else. When we avoid pain, struggle not to feel it, pain turns into suffering.

There is an enormous difference between pain and suffering. Pain often cannot be avoided. Suffering can. As we learn the difference between them, many fears subside.

As we practice, thought subsides and we become one with the sound of the birds, the heat of summer, the smile of a friend, the feeling of soapy dishwater on your hands. Thinking takes us away from that. But direct experience will bring us all the healing, joy, and strength needed for everything.

The Zendo

Silence is the beginning of healing. The zendo is a space dedicated to silence—to Zen meditation. It can be huge, a monastery that holds many, a simple temple, a country shed, a tree house, or it can also be a special part of your own apartment. Usually it is kept clean and empty, with a few flowers and a cushion to sit on. This will be described in detail in a future chapter.

From the moment we enter the zendo, we are silent. All usual social greetings and communications are suspended as we leave our social selves behind at the door. We do not have to pretend to be who we aren't, to be happy when we're sad, to be strong when we're feeling vulnerable. We come to the zendo to practice. We do not come to make demands on anyone else. Unless we are at teatime, or at other times requiring social interaction, we do not look at each other, or seek recognition or approval. This is the time for making acquaintance with our own Self.

Communication with others develops differently as we sit in silence. It becomes deep, profound, and lasting. We speak and are spoken to in different ways. Bells, clappers, and gongs announce the beginning and end of activities. After a period of sitting, we perform jobs assigned to us, such as cleaning and cooking, with 100 percent of ourselves. This is our communication.

After spending several days sitting beside someone during a silent meditation retreat, you know all there is to know about that person, and feel as close to him or her as to yourself, even though the two of you haven't spoken. Finally, it is easy to realize that our words, actions, and false mannerisms, rather than bringing us closer to one another, can serve as walls to keep others away. At this time you begin to know what it means to "go home and be kind to your patient," and to actualize the command—to love your neighbor as yourself.

> All beings are flowers
> Blooming
> In a blooming universe.
> —*Soen Nakagawa Roshi*

CHAPTER 2

How to Do It

ZEN MIRACLE 2
*No more leaning on others,
you can depend on yourself.*

How to Do It: Zen Meditation

In Zen practice it is said that the best instruction is no instruction, the best encouragement is no encouragement. This forces you to cut the depending mind, find out for yourself, and stand on your own two feet.

If one has the opportunity, it is wonderful to go to a zendo, practice with others, and receive guidance and encouragement. For those who cannot do this, however, it is also possible to practice on your own. This practice is ultimately yours and can be done anywhere you choose. There is no difference in what you do when you are sitting in a zendo and sitting at home. Begin wherever you are. As you do, new possibilities may appear in your life. Ultimately, when the practice grows ripe enough, the whole world becomes your zendo and wherever you go, you are at home.

Create a Space

In order to create a space for sitting in your home or apartment, you will need to do a few things. First, remove all clutter from a part of your home. Create a clean, empty space. Then get a cushion to sit on (in Zen centers there are large, square cushions with small, round ones on top of them). In your home, any comfortable cushion will do to start. (If you cannot sit on a cushion, a straight-backed chair will do.) Some enjoy having a little bell beside them to announce the beginning and end of sittings, along with a stick of incense to burn. Fresh flowers and water can add to the atmosphere. Your environment affects your meditation, and your meditation affects your environment.

As you create space in your physical world, your inner world will open as well. The emptier the space you create to sit in, the bigger your world will become.

Take Your Shoes Off

Usually we never pay attention to our feet. They are taken for granted, covered up with socks and shoes. When we take all of these coverings off, we realize that our feet are among the most sensitive parts of our bodies. Filled with nerve endings, they connect us to the ground we walk on, as well as to what's going on inside; they are able to absorb wisdom and information we could not receive any other way.

When we enter a zendo, the first thing we do is take off our shoes and place them neatly in a rack by the door. First, we do not want to trek dust and dirt through the zendo, which is always immaculately clean; but more important, we take off our shoes because our feet are precious. We honor and respect our feet, and walk on them carefully. We do not discard what they have to teach. Zen practice is just like this. Nothing discarded, everything used in the way it was intended. We walk slowly, eyes on the floor, concentrating on each step, feeling the floor under our feet as we approach our seat.

Sit Down

Sit down on your cushion on the floor (a chair will also do), cross your legs, keep your back straight, hold your neck up, and look down with eyes opened. Eyes are open because we do not want to fall asleep or go into dreams. Zen is the practice of waking up, of knowing when we are fantasizing, and when we are here, right now.

This is different from other forms of meditation. Zazen does not involve trying to reach any particular state, but simply waking up to what already is. We do not have to create anything special, only learn how to be present with whatever presents itself to us, moment by moment, breath by breath.

Cup your left hand next to your navel, cup your right hand beneath the left and touch both thumbs together. Then, put your mind or attention in the place beneath your navel—your *Hara*, or vital center.

"Is that all there is to it?" David asked after his first period of instruction. "I was let down. I expected it to take me to the stars. It took me a long time to realize that the stars are right here, with every breath."

Do Not Lean on Anything

Posture is important. Do not lean on anything. In this practice we learn to not lean, but to discover and depend on our own original balance and strength. If you can sit in lotus, half lotus, or simply cross-legged posture, this is helpful. If you can't, don't worry. Do your best and the zazen will take care of everything else. All you have to be concerned about is holding the posture as best you can. (You can also sit with your legs folded beneath you, the cushion in-between.)

As you stop leaning in your practice, you will also stop leaning and wobbling in other areas of your life. You will stop demanding that others take care of you, or stop pretending you are too weak to look after your own life. One of the greatest treasures of Zen practice is finding your own natural strength.

Breathe

To begin the sitting, count your breath from one to ten. After ten, start again at one, following your natural breath. Don't interfere with that. Don't make it anything special. (This instruction is fine for the first fifty years.) Later, a teacher may give other practices to do—or may not. That is not important now. For now, the important thing is to sit regularly, for as long as you can.

LET A LONG BREATH BE LONG, AND A SHORT BREATH BE SHORT

As you sit, do not worry about your breathing. Do not worry about anything. Usually we rush through the day filled with thoughts, plans, anger, sorrow, and all the while we're receiving this incredible breath, moment by moment. We're not grateful for it, don't acknowledge it's there, or consider what would happen if it stopped for a few moments. But each breath is given freely. Each breath is fine just as it is. Let a long breath be long, a short breath be short. After you receive it, simply exhale, and give it back. You are allowing yourself to finally realize that you're actually alive right now. As you pay attention to your breathing, your life has no choice but to turn around.

WHEN THE BELL RINGS, LISTEN TO THE BELL

A bell rings out three times to announce the beginning of a sitting. When the bell rings, listen to it. When it stops ringing, listen to that. How often do we listen to the sounds around us, or hear the silence when the sounds end? How often do we listen to the words of others, hear the cries beneath their voices? Most of us live our lives deaf to the calls made upon us. Here we stop and listen. As practice goes on, listening grows deeper until we can finally hear the sounds of silence, and beyond.

> Listen to the one who is listening.
> —*Master Bankei*

Do Not Move

Once the sitting begins, do not move until it ends. A sitting can last for as long or short a period of time as you desire. In Zen centers, sittings range from thirty minutes to an hour—or more. Five-, ten-, or fifteen-minute sittings at home for beginners are also fine. Do what you can. The important thing is regularity. The practice builds up in its own time and way.

Not moving during a sitting is very important. Usually, the moment we feel uncomfortable we want to move, to fix or change the discomfort. By not moving, we stop our habitual reactions and allow ourselves to just be present with whatever arises. When thoughts come, do not repress or hate them, just notice what is there, and return to breathing—return to the present moment. Thoughts come and go; there is no need to attach to them. Reactions come and go as well. Sometimes we feel deep love, other times hate. Sometimes we wish to live completely, other times life seems unbearable. We do not allow ourselves to be at the mercy of passing phenomena. Instead, we allow ourselves to experience all that arises—and then let it go.

Usually when we suffer we try to fix, to improve, to analyze ourselves. Some want to change the world as well. To change, heal, and repair the world is the cornerstone of many religious traditions. But in Zen we ask, "Where is the world? Who is this Self you are fixing?"

The Buddha said, "To straighten another, do a harder thing— first straighten yourself." (*Dhammapada*) Before you run around trying to heal the world, your boyfriend, your marriage, your mother, your father, wait a minute. Sit down and straighten yourself.

Over and Over

In Zen we do the same things a hundred times and more. Learn to love repetition. A raindrop that falls on a piece of rock may have to fall a thousand times before the rock becomes a little softer and can absorb the rain. The same is true for our minds and hearts. Over and over we hear the same raindrop in the zendo, the same gong, the same bell, the same clappers, the same instruction. We sit down, day after day, in the same way and we stop moving, chasing, fixing, thinking. We no longer run away from our pain or act it out. Instead, we allow ourselves to be with whatever is going on without judgments. Then, whatever has arisen passes, and we have to be with something else. Then that passes and something else appears.

As we do this, we're actually pulling the plug on our suffering, taking our attention back from the outside world, and returning it to ourselves. Zen is the practice of returning you to yourself.

Pay Attention

Where our attention is, our life is—our energy. Now it is time to take back our attention from the endless phenomena and stimuli that claim it, to pay attention to what is happening within. Dreams, memories, fears, fantasies, commands—they lose their power to control us. As sitting continues, we see them for what they are. Our choices, actions, and responses then become appropriate to the present situation, to what is actually happening now.

All of this happens simply by our paying attention to our breath, to this very moment. We watch or feel the breath come in, and then feel it go out. For some, this seems inconsequential. *Where will that get me?* they ask. They do not realize that, without this very breath, they would not be able to live at all.

As we practice, our priorities shift. That which we thought was inconsequential, such as the next breath, becomes precious. That which we thought was so urgently needed, such as the next boyfriend or new car, becomes less pressing. We can do without more and more. We are not using others, ourselves, or the goods the world provides to "make" our lives right. As we sit, we see how our lives are already right. And we say thank you.

GET UP WHEN THE TIME COMES

The bell rings at the end of a period of zazen, which means the sitting is over. (If you are alone, you can ring it yourself.) After we hear the bell, we put our hands together and make a little bow. Then we stand, even if we want to keep on sitting. All activities are done in unison. We do not call attention to ourselves. The strength of the *Sangha* (group of people sitting together), is *our* strength as well. As we act in harmony and give to the Sangha, we simultaneously receive.

Even when we have resistance to doing the next activity, we have no choice but to just do what has to be done. This itself is a wonderful teaching. We do not linger with that which is over. Although we fear or resist what comes next, we simply take the necessary action—enter into the next activity. Once we are in action, most fear and resistance dissipates of itself.

After we get up and walk around, we sit down again, but we don't know what we're sitting down into—it could be heaven or it could be hell. Whatever it is, it has a time limit. The bell will ring again. Once again we will get up and walk. Then, when that's over, once again we will sit down. In life, we can get stuck in something and wonder if the bell is ever going to ring. Is the situation ever going to be over? Sometimes we're so stuck, it feels as if the bell hasn't rung for fifty years. Here, it helps us to get up, walk, and realize that everything passes in time.

PAY ATTENTION TO EACH STEP YOU TAKE

Kinhin is walking meditation. After a period of sitting, of gathering our energy and concentration, we get up and resume activity. Rather than plunging into this activity mindlessly, we take the focus and awareness that has developed during the sitting and put it into what we do next.

Kinhin can last from five to fifteen minutes or more. During kinhin, we walk slowly, one behind the other, hands clasped under our breastbone, back straight, eyes down, paying attention to the bottom of our feet and to our breathing. We pay attention to each step as we take it. That's all. We are not walking to get somewhere, but to be exactly where we are. Each step is precious and unique. As we walk it becomes clear that, *"This particular step will not come again."*

At the end of kinhin, two wooden clappers sound to announce that kinhin is coming to an end. We put our hands together and, in a line, walk back to our cushion. The clappers sound again; we bow and sit down for the next period of zazen.

Put Your Hands Together and Bow

We put our hands together many times during Zen practice. This is called *gassho*. In doing this we bring all parts of ourselves together—left and right, good and bad, masculine and feminine. We unite the world of opposites, the dualistic world. Putting our hands together also contributes to our focus; most important, it is a way to express our thanks and acknowledgment, to stop and say thank you to everything—to the room for being here, to the cushions and bells, to others who have come to offer their presence and support.

This moment of recognition is crucial. When we carry this mindfulness and gratitude throughout our day, everything appears different.

When the Time Comes to Go—Go

It is difficult to leave when the time comes to go. No one wants to say good-bye. Coming and going are the nature of our lives, but we all think we are here permanently, whether in a home, relationship, or stage of life. We have no idea of what the next stage, person, or moment is bringing. We make up ideas, beliefs, dreams, and fantasies to secure our future. Though this is natural, deep down we base our hopes upon fictions. Fundamentally, we know that this is so and live in hope, fear, worry, and expectation.

Zen practice establishes our lives upon an entirely different basis. Though we may not want to leave, and do not know what's coming next, when the time comes to go, we simply go. We just take the next step, focusing completely on where we are now. When our hearts and minds are present to the moment, there is no room for projected fears of the future or memories of the past to intrude. This moment is always sufficient in itself.

> A Lord asked Master Takuan, a Zen teacher, how he might spend the time. He felt his days very long attending his office and sitting stiffly to receive visitors. Master Takuan wrote eight Chinese characters and gave them to the man:
>
> > Not twice this day
> > Inch time foot gem.
> > This day will not come again.
> > Each minute is worth a priceless gem.
>
> > —*Zen Flesh, Zen Bones*

No Failure or Success

Many feel uneasy as they start to practice, wondering if they are doing it correctly. But if you follow the simple instructions, you cannot make a mistake. You can do nothing wrong. Whatever happens during that particular sitting is perfect, just as it is. All you need to do is experience it. There is no way you can fail. Someone might say, "I had a horrible sitting," or, "I had a horrible day." But you haven't had a horrible sitting. You may have had discomfort, but calling it horrible is extra. You simply had what you had. You survived. You sat there and breathed, and felt what happened.

Someone else might say, "I had such a beautiful sitting, I was in bliss, I was one with everyone in the zendo." But then the next sitting, he or she is back into something else. It's not a matter of clinging to anything, it's a microcosm of daily life and we learn a new way of dealing with it.

For those who want fast results and instant gratification, this practice can be difficult. These people operate under the illusion that *they* are the ones who do everything in life, that *they* are in charge—they can fix life, change it. Zen practice says, "Not exactly." Though there's nothing you can do wrong, there's nothing you can do right, either. It is not a matter of failure or success. Actually, zazen is not something *you* are doing. You are just following instructions. The zazen does everything itself.

> If you only do this simple practice, day by day, step by step, breath by breath, it is impossible to fail. Just the way your foot cannot fail to hit the floor when it takes a step on it, if you continue this practice, you cannot fail one day, to wake up.
> —*Soen Nakagawa Roshi*

PRACTICE

Soen Roshi, a great twentieth-century Zen Master who died in 1984, former abbot of Ryutakaji Monastery, is speaking about practice, also called *Gyo*. For many, there is a dichotomy between sitting and living, or being in action; however, these are like two wings of a bird, both needed to navigate through the sky.

Real practice encompasses every moment of our lives—waking, sleeping, speaking, loving, and being in the marketplace. At all times and in all places we remain wakeful and vigilant. We do everything with a full body, mind, and heart. True practice is living from all of yourself.

ZEN IN ACTION

Exercise 1: Return to the Source

In the midst of speaking, working, cleaning, or any other activity, stop a moment. Pay attention to where you are, and to your breathing. Actively take your attention back from the external world and follow your breath. Do this at least three times a day.

Exercise 2: Feel the Air on Your Face

As you are in the heat of pursuit, anger, or strong emotion, stop and do nothing. Watch yourself. Ask what all the excitement is about. Notice your posture, breathing, and responses. Straighten your back. Feel your feet upon the floor. Feel the air on your face. Realize you have been caught in a momentary thunderstorm. Maintain stillness until it blows away.

> At last
> I have met
> My own cool star.
> —*Soen Nakagawa Roshi*

CHAPTER 3

WELCOME TO THE WORLD OF KOANS

ZEN MIRACLE 3
*You find both your questions
and answers right where you are.*

During Rinzai Zen practice the Master will present *koans* to his students. Along with zazen, koans are the heart of Rinzai Zen. These koans are Zen questions that cannot be answered rationally or logically, but must be responded to with your entire life. Initially when you hear a koan, it may have no meaning—you may be stumped and feel as though your mind has turned into a cloud of mud, entirely useless. That's a good beginning.

BRING ME A BOWL
WITHOUT USING YOUR HANDS

For example, the master may tell the student, "Bring me a bowl without using your hands," or, "Cross the mountain without moving an inch." Just as life itself presents impossible situations that require solutions we cannot think of, koans push us beyond our usual obsessive rumination into a wide, open place.

In order to bring a living answer, the koan forces you to tap into unknown parts of your being. You must grab onto the koan and work with it relentlessly until it becomes your flesh and bones. Soon you are not working on the koan, it is working on you. In the process dualistic thought is put to an end, right and wrong become meaningless, personal strategies have no bearing and the constant worry about passing or failing all begin to die down. This itself finally frees us to find new solutions to life.

During work on koans we are confronted with our "imagined" difficulties and limitations. A koan can be solved in an instant or it can be worked on for years. The odd thing about koans is that even when they are solved in an instant, we still must continue working on them for years. We can pass them one day, and fail the next. Delusions are strong, ingrained habits can acquire a life of their own.

The deeper we dig into our koan, the more we find that the paradoxes and conflicts of life do not trap us as much. We become at home with confusion and complication, not trying to solve them in the same way. We are not so forceful about imposing our view of life upon the vast, mysterious world. Little by little, the black-and-white world we had lived in before begins to turn into thousands of shades of gray—and blue, purple, amethyst. There is no end to the color and beauty we find.

You Are the Answer

We usually feel that the answer to a problem is somewhere outside, apart from ourselves. We search for it avidly and feel like failures if the solution to our questions does not become clear. On the other hand, if we do find a temporary solution, we cling to it mercilessly, thinking it will always be correct. Somehow we do not realize that as conditions change, our solutions, too, may lose their reality, may no longer be suitable.

Koan practice shakes us free of this. In order to solve the koan, we must realize where it comes from, find the One who is questioning. Rather than fix our attention upon the intricacies of the question, we turn to Who is craving the answer. As soon as this is discovered, the solution is immensely clear. Some laugh very hard at this moment. Others have a good cry.

The very process of answering a koan is itself the answer. Sitting with it, sleeping with it, chewing it as you chew your food, this koan becomes your own self. As you continue being with it unconditionally, an answer appears at the perfect moment, just like a baby chick bursting out of its shell.

No Imitations

The answer that you bring to the master cannot be a copy of anyone else's. It must be *yours*. Someone else's answer isn't your answer—someone else's life isn't your life.

So many of us live counterfeit lives, wanting only to fulfill some image we or someone else has about the kind of person we should become. Zen practice asks you not to worry about who you "should" become. Find out who you are right now.

Basically, we have no idea of who it is we really are, or what will make our lives complete. In this frame of mind we cannot even begin to approach a koan. First we have to remove the masks that separate us from ourselves. Doing this we break through our own barriers, encounter our own heart, mind, blood, guts.

> I received my first koan from my teacher during my first retreat. I went up to his room for private interview and the moment I saw him sitting there was struck dumb, unable to say a word. He sat silently, waiting. In horror at my stupidity, I stared, baffled.
>
> It took two years to pass that first koan. Every time I receive a new one, I react exactly the same way.
>
> —*Andrew, Zen student*

Different koans address various aspects of Zen practice. *The Gateless Gate*, and *Blue Cliff Records* are two classical collections of koans presented by great Zen Masters of the past. Along with the koan, there is commentary and usually a verse. Other Zen Masters give *teishos* (Zen talks given during retreats), and exhortations based upon the koans. Everything presents a glimpse of the koan from a slightly different point of view. But if you try to understand this rationally, you will be lost. To break through a koan, zazen is needed.

A long-term Zen student, Miro Lisa Clark speaks about how her work with koans transformed her entire life.

A Moment of Lucidity

At some point in my practice of zazen, suicide stopped being an option. Once, on my fortieth birthday, I noticed that I had weathered half a lifetime, more or less. Why not put aside the option of just stopping my indifferent role in today's business and the next day's? However, at that time forsaking the rational option of suicide was still too scary. Gradually the concept faded away. Nonetheless, it is a miracle that I hadn't just walked off the edge of the earth by then.

Sometimes pain precedes or is the essence of a moment of lucidity within Zen practice. A turning point for me occurred in the aftermath of physical pain, when incidentally, I did take myself to a sesshin and went to dokusan (a meeting with the Zen Master).

Pneumonia—it would not have been so serious if my lungs weren't already ridged with scar tissue. Watching my breath was no help. To breathe was sheer pain. A white spot kept me still. The image was more visceral than visual. Intense stillness braced me for the inevitable cough that would blast my ribs but bring the inhalation I could not bear to gently pull in. First surprise: Why did I work so hard not to close down? Second surprise: Why was my Zen Master, equally friend and stranger listening to this personal stuff, clarifying?

His words were a nexus. "The white spot must be Life," he said.

A new, finer exhalation of understanding. The white spot began to melt and diffuse in synch with my recovery over the next eight or nine weeks.

Did he save my life? Not from pneumonia, though his words and care were medicine. But how interesting! What a new koan life became! A present in which true beginnings, moments of insight pop right before you—no digging through layers of memory along paths of association.

But such shifts in awareness need not be arrived at painfully. For instance, a few years later: the "moment" of the golden day—what else can I call it? Waking at dawn, all forms were porous, impalpable. A "full circle of radiance" gave up any form whatsoever: easy, buoyant light was spread throughout consciousness from dawn through a workday into evening zazen: A present as fresh as the next exhalation. This is always available to me—for a flash. But, if I try to extend that moment, hold onto it, examine the feeling, the vision, the silence, it hardens into a lifeless fossil. Better to be freshly empty, to know that each such deepening subtly changes all awareness from now on.

From this point on Miro's life took a new turn. It was not that she didn't have problems to deal with, conflicts and struggles, times of loneliness, but that the "full circle of radiance" she had discovered remained with her throughout, guiding, prompting, and providing a larger context for her to hold her experience in.

ZEN IN ACTION

Exercise 1: Catching Your Koan

Take a problem you are dealing with in life that seems difficult or insoluble to you at the moment and realize it is a koan. Stop trying to figure or work it out. Approach it differently. Sit with it, be with it, make friends with all aspects of it. Find out where it originates from and who the One is who needs it to be solved. Stop longing for a solution. Realize that this koan, just as it is now, is your very lifeblood.

Joshu was one of the great Zen Masters of ancient China during the T'ang dynasty who lived from 778–897. His greatness as a teacher can be seen in prevalence of many of his sayings in the great koan anthologies. As Fukushima Roshi, the present-day abbot of Tokufuji Monastery, says, "Joshu is one of the great examples of authentic Patriarch Zen, as the Zen brought from India to China by Bodhidharma (the founder of Zen) is called."

The first koan usually given to students is Joshu's MU. This koan is vast and includes all others. Some work on no other koan than this one for years. After they answer it, their masters may advise them: "Go back and work on it now for another thirty years."

Then what? Work on it yourself and find out.

Most of the koans students work with are included in the *Mumonkan* (*The Gateless Gate*) and *Hekiganroku* (*The Blue Cliff Records*), which are among the classics in the literature of Zen, and from which I'm quoting. Composed in China in the Sung dynasty (960–1279), they are collections of the most frequently studied koans. Mumonkan was compiled by the Zen monk Mumon Ekai and is a collection of forty-eight koans, to each of which Mumon added a comment and a verse.

The *Hekiganroku* (*The Blue Cliff Records*) was composed about a hundred years earlier, a collection of 100 koans compiled by Setcho (980–1052), an outstanding Zen Master and poet. About a century later another Zen Master, Engo (1063–1135), added comments on the main subject.

CASE 1: (FROM *MUMONKAN*—
TRANSLATED AS *THE GATELESS GATE*)

A monk asked Joshu, "Has a dog the Buddha Nature?"
Joshu answered, "Mu."

(Buddha Nature is original nature, and MU can be translated to mean No, or Nothing.)

Koan: What is MU?

MUMON'S COMMENT

"In order to master Zen, you must pass the barrier of the patriarchs. To attain this subtle realization, you must completely cut off the way of thinking. If you do not pass the barrier, and do not cut off the way of thinking, then you will be like a ghost clinging to the bushes and weeds. Now, I want to ask you, what is the barrier of the patriarchs? Why is it this single word MU? If you pass through it, not only will you be able to see Joshu face to face, but you will also go hand in hand with the successive patriarchs, seeing with the same eyes, hearing with the same ears. Isn't that a delightful prospect? Wouldn't you like to pass this barrier?

"Arouse your entire body; summon up a spirit of great doubt and concentrate on this word 'Mu.' Carry it continuously day and night. Do not form a nihilistic conception of vacancy or a relative conception of has or has not. It will be just as if you swallow a red-hot iron ball, which you cannot spit out even if you try. All the illusory ideas and delusive thoughts accumulated up to the present will be exterminated, and when the time comes, internal and external will be spontaneously united. You will know this, but for yourself only, like a dumb man who has had a dream. Then all of a sudden an explosive conversion will occur, and you will astonish the heavens and shake the earth.

"Now, I want to ask you again, "How will you carry it out?" Employ every ounce of your energy to work on this "Mu." If you hold on without interruption, behold: a single spark, and the holy candle is lit!"

MUMON'S VERSE

> The dog, the Buddha Nature,
> The pronouncement, perfect and final.
> Before you say it has or has not,
> You are a dead man on the spot.

Are you a dead person, or fully alive? Can you see MU?

CHAPTER 4

PEELING ONIONS DAY BY DAY

ZEN MIRACLE 4
You become able to peel an onion, completely.

Master Dogen, who was born in 1200 in Kyoto and died in 1253, is the founder of the Soto Zen School, which does not use koans, but focuses upon simple sitting and work. Living at a time when Zen was in decline in Japan, Dogen traveled to China, visiting the major monasteries. Finally after two years, he came upon his teacher Rujing, with whom he trained.

When Dogen Zenji arrived at the monastery in China he found an old monk working hard in the garden in the hot sun, drying out mushrooms. Feeling badly that this old monk was working so hard, Dogen asked if he could help him. The old monk refused.

"This is my work," he told Dogen. "Who will do it if I don't?"

This beautiful old monk taught Dogen true practice. He had learned the value of doing his work, knowing that no one else could do it for him, or exactly as he could. Most important, he realized that his work was a privilege for him. He understood the powerful fact that everyday life is practice, doing one's work fully, day by day.

Most feel that work is a privilege when they gain position over another, earn large sums of money, or are publicly acclaimed.

These are all ways of receiving value from the consequences of work, not from the job itself. The old monk that Dogen met received his sense of value simply from doing what was needed. No job was too large or too small.

TAKE CARE OF THE WORLD YOU LIVE IN

Zen practice focuses upon tasks that are ordinary. Anyone can do them. Everyone must. Each task must be done thoroughly, impeccably, not rushed through to get to the next. One task is not more important than the other, just like one person is not more important than the next. Birds, insects, animals, are cared for and respected equally. All of life is precious and whatever presents itself is cared for. We do not sift out one thing from another. Also, we do not do something hoping for a reward. That is adding something extra. This something extra causes anguish if it does not arrive.

Scott, a fifty-year-old physician, lived his entire life in a whirl of work. He graduated first in his class from medical school, undertook a rigorous internship, and built a huge practice, which took all his time. When he suddenly suffered a severe heart attack, he lost his grounding. Grasping at life with each breath, all he longed for those moments, was to be able to breathe one more time. Each breath became like honey. At that moment, his momentous accomplishments could do nothing for him—they faded to nothing before his eyes. It was life itself that he longed for. He realized at that intense time, that he had never valued life before.

Daily life, our simple breath, is our training ground. This is also called *ordinary mind*.

> To have some deep feeling about Buddhism is not the point; we just do what we should do, like eating supper and going to bed. This is Buddhism.
>
> —*Suzuki-roshi*

DAILY TASKS

Just the way everyday life repeats itself, just the way we get up every morning and go to bed every night, so Zen practice, too, focuses upon tasks of daily life that repeat themselves naturally—breathing, washing, sitting, standing, raking leaves, peeling onions for the soup when we need them.

Most consider these events insignificant, something to do and get over with fast. They are irritating chores we'd rather allocate to others, while we think great thoughts or do "important work" that is designed to save the world. We are eager to take on complicated projects that give a sense of accomplishment. But no matter how much we accomplish or do not accomplish, our suffering and loneliness still go on.

Here we learn that we don't have to be fancy or smart. We don't have to be anything. All we have to be able to do is to sit down. Can we sit down? Fine. Can we breathe? Great—a top student. Do we know how to listen when the bell rings? Can we hear it? Wonderful. Can we get up when it's time to get up? That's all we need to know. Can we manage to persevere? Actually, that is all we need to do.

PRESSURE TO MAKE THE GRADE

Many come from a background where there is so much pressure to make the grade, to succeed, to be impressive, that for them, this practice is a much needed relief. To sit when they sit, stand when they stand—not have to constantly focus on achieving something.

Psychologically speaking, when an individual is living under the pressure to constantly achieve, a subtle message is communicated—that he or she is not enough, not loveable just as they are. Love and value must be earned. Of course this is never experienced as love or true nourishment. No matter how much praise or love such an individual seems to receive, deep down they feel that it is only their achievements that are being cared for, not them.

As we practice, however, we grow to realize that we are sufficient as we are, more than sufficient, whole and complete. Rather than seek glory, we realize that everyday life itself, breathing and peeling onions *are* sufficient in themselves as well. However, most of the time we have not been available to them, we've been somewhere else. As we return to the moment and to the daily facts of our lives, to onions that need peeling, to wash that must be done, we are returning to the essence of life itself. Why throw this away for a mirage of glory we are only dreaming of? Daily life itself is complete. It deserves full attention. When we do this fully, suffering is over. We are complete and content right where we are.

The Zen Garden

A famous dignitary was coming to visit a Zen monastery and intense preparations were being made for the visit. The Zen Master instructed the monks to carefully rake up all the leaves that had fallen over their beautiful rock garden. The monks gave particular attention to this task as this garden was a source of great acclaim. The task was completed perfectly about half an hour before the visit.

The Zen Master then went to a deck that was directly above the garden to inspect the outcome of the monks' work. He saw that every leaf had been raked, all the weeds removed, and the rocks hosed down so that they were gleaming in the sun. Some of the monks down below saw him inspecting the garden. They had completed the work just in time.

After the Master was satisfied with their work, he left for a moment and then returned with a huge bag of old leaves. To the monks' horror and without a moment's notice, he immediately tossed them down all over the garden again.

"Now this is a perfect Zen garden," said the Master. "Don't forget that."

The master was teaching the monks that work itself suffices, to forget about results. Whatever life brings is perfect. One cannot improve upon that.

DON'T DEPEND ON RESULTS

Psychologically speaking, the Zen Master withdrew the satisfaction the monks could have attained for their efforts. Some might call this nihilism, saying that effort doesn't matter. Their efforts did matter, but in an entirely different way. It mattered that they were involved and engaged. It mattered that they did their best each moment. It also mattered that they could accept whatever consequences came.

Speaking from a larger vantage point, satisfaction obtained from specific results is fleeting, and dependent upon circumstances. The master was teaching the monks not to depend upon results for fulfillment; that, in the long run, human efforts do not bring true perfection.

Psychologically speaking, the more we confront disappointment, confusion, and loneliness, the more we seek complicated methods of alleviating them. As our solutions become more sophisticated, layers are added to our suffering. Soon we forget the original problem and are caught in a secondary maze of dilemmas caused by the solutions themselves. In many cases the medicine we are taking, and its side effects, are more dangerous than the original disease.

For those who want great glory, this practice may seem to fall short. They do not realize that glory is already present in each moment of life. Being available to live in this manner is glory itself. Making extraordinary efforts to be more than others is far off the point. All we must do is persevere.

PERSEVERE

"If you lose the spirit of repetition, your practice will become quite difficult," Suzuki-roshi says. Most of training goes to teach us perseverance, especially sesshin, the intense training periods.

SESSHIN—INTENSE TRAINING PERIODS

Sesshin is an intense training period, of either one day, three days, seven days, three months, or sometimes more. From morning until night we do nothing but practice. This is a great teaching in perseverance, going on and getting through each day's schedule no matter how we feel. Life itself can also be considered a sesshin, where we must go on no matter what.

Usually we wake at four or so in the morning and continue until nine or ten at night. Along with intense zazen practice, there is time for daily work. Some of the jobs a student does are washing dishes, mopping floors, cleaning toilets, lining up the cushions exactly, making sure the water for the flowers is fresh. One task is not regarded as more significant than another. No person is too important to do any kind of job. No matter how much pain, annoyance, or boredom comes, no matter how much we are resisting, we just continue on and on.

At one of my early sesshins, it was evening of the third day of retreat. We had been sitting in zazen for seventeen hours a day. By now the pain was almost unbearable and I was exhausted and bored. My legs and back were aching and I wanted to go home. Then came time for evening sitting, which lasted a good hour. I didn't think I could make it.

I sat down on my cushion and the bells rang out to begin. After the bells, absolute silence. Soon the pain began to mount. There was no way I could escape it. The more I fought, the worse it became. Beside myself, I broke the silence and started sobbing loudly. Although I was disturbing others I couldn't stop. The more I cried, the worse I felt. Still, I could not go on.

Then, to my horror, the head monk Dogo bellowed at me. "Shut up or get out. Go and sit by yourself down at the lake. There is no pain. You are the pain. Become stronger than the pain."

At that moment I stopped crying. The pain went. I went. Instead there was incredible joy.

ORDINARY MOMENTS

Just as we think we need to create perfect gardens or lives, we also think spirituality is about moments of great revelation, peak experiences, personal ecstasy. While these moments, when they come, are precious, they can also be nothing more than a drug, removing us from what needs to be done—sitting through a painful sitting, keeping quiet so as not to disturb others, taking care of those who are needy, attending to that which is right in front of our eyes.

Suzuki-roshi, the Zen Master who died in 1971, abbot of San Francisco Zen Center and author of *Zen Mind, Beginner's Mind*, focuses a great deal upon the simplicity of practice, not adding anything extra to it. "If your practice is good, you may become proud of it. What you do is good, but something extra more is added to it. Pride is extra. Right effort is to get rid of something extra."

What he is saying is that the right effort is to get rid of pride. Putting full attention to ordinary life, to simple moments, diminishes our ego. We realize that life is already miraculous and we become concerned with doing what we are doing, not building our false selves up. By not trying to take charge of anything, a strange thing happens—we become the master of circumstances, no longer in their grip.

THE SIMPLE MIND

The modern-day Zen Master Joko Charlotte Beck, currently head of the San Diego Zen Center and author of *Everyday Zen*, says, "Awareness is completely simple; we don't have to add any-thing to it to change it. It is unassuming or unpretentious; it can't help but be that way. Awareness is not a thing, to be affected by this or that. When we live from pure awareness, we are not affected by our past, our present, or our future. Because awareness has nothing it can pretend to, it's humble. It's lowly. It's simple."

As we apply simple awareness both to our questions and to the everyday tasks before us we learn to persevere in practice, develop a taste for boredom, or repetition, and not run to imagination. Most of us must do or hear a thing a thousand times before we are able to break out of the fog we are living in. The ongoingness of practice builds momentum. It makes it a part of our natural, daily routine.

When we focus our simple awareness upon daily tasks, the false self has no place to take hold, and ego, which causes so much anguish, gives way to something else. As well as being great med-icine, this daily practice of doing what needs to be done—sweep-ing the floor, washing your plate after you've eaten, walking to the beach with someone who needs you—is the practice of car-ing for life. No questions asked. No hesitation. The benefits to all beings, and to yourself as well, are infinite.

ZEN IN ACTION

Exercise 1: Peel an Onion

Peel an onion. Peel it again. And again. Peel some more. Keep peeling. Notice everything that's happening as you peel on and on.

Boring? Annoying? Why? Are you searching for something? Trying to get to the core? Forget it. Just peel. Your responses are irrelevant. Watch them come and go. Do you base your life upon transitory responses like these? What have these kinds of responses really done to your life?

Keep peeling the onion. When there is nothing left to peel, peel some more.

Who's peeling? Where's the onion? What's all this about?

Exercise 2: Pick Up Your Coat from the Floor

What's lying around unattended to in your home or life? Pick it up right now and put it in its rightful place. Is it a piece of clothing, paper, toothbrush, person, relationship? Is it an old dream that has been hanging there a long time? Just pick it up, wash or dust it off and put it where it belongs.

Exercise 3: Persevere

Enjoy persevering at something. Pick one activity that requires a great deal of perseverance and do it for a designated amount of time every day this week. Whether or not you are in the mood to do it, do it anyway. When the time is over, put it down. Then pick it up the next day. See what happens as a result of this to you, and to the activity.

CASE 19: (FROM *MUMONKAN*—TRANSLATED AS *THE GATELESS GATE*)

Koan: Ordinary Mind Is the Way

Joshu asked Nansen, "What is the Way?"

"Ordinary mind is the way," Nansen replied.

"Shall I try to seek after it?" Joshu asked.

"If you try to seek after it, you will become separated from it," responded Nansen.

"How can I know the way unless I try for it?" persisted Joshu.

Nansen said, "The Way is not a matter of knowing or not knowing. Knowing is delusion; not knowing is confusion. When you have really reached the true Way beyond doubt, you will find it as vast and boundless as outer space. How can it be talked about on a level of right or wrong?"

With those words, Joshu came to a sudden realization.

MUMON'S COMMENT

"Nansen dissolved and melted away before Joshu's questions, and could not offer a plausible explanation. Even though Joshu comes to a realization, he must delve into it for another thirty years before he can fully understand it."

MUMON'S VERSE

The spring flowers, the autumn moon;
Summer breezes, winter snow.
If useless things do not clutter your mind,
You have the best days of your life.

CHAPTER 5

DOING NOTHING

ZEN MIRACLE 5
"Spring comes and the flowers grow by themselves."

GO BACK TO KINDERGARTEN

The most dangerous thing in the world is to think you understand something.

—Lao Tzu

Most of us feel we must be so smart, learn more and more, do better, be faster, make our latest achievements outdistance those of the past. We're in a race with ourselves that is never over, and no matter how fast we run, we never really arrive anywhere.

As we do Zen practice, we reverse our momentum, go back to kindergarten, in order to realize that no matter how intelligent we may have become, we do not know the first thing about being content in daily life. We also begin to realize we know very little about how to help another grow.

Ted, a Zen student who has been practicing for over thirty years, remembered the first time he became interested in practice. He had gone to attend a lecture on Zen. When he walked into the room there were many students present, chatting with one another. A Zen monk, Taisani, stood completely still in front of the room. The chatting continued and the monk waited. Finally, the chatting died down and the room became still. Before speaking, the monk looked down for a moment and noticed that one of his shoelaces was untied. He bent over slowly, paying attention to nothing in the world except tying his shoelace, as if it was the most important thing in the world.

"It was amazing watching him," said Ted. "That second I was hooked. I wondered, *Who is this guy?* Just by tying his shoelace he was able to hold us all spellbound."

The Master of Circumstances

All of our frantic activity is an attempt to master circumstances, control anxiety, get what we want, feel as though we are in charge.

How do we master circumstances? Psychologically speaking, we usually plan, plot, examine all variables, control others, agonize. A great deal of therapy is devoted to knowing what we "want," and how to "get it," learning how to empower ourselves in the world. Ego structures are developed to cope with others, defenses are put in place, life trajectories are developed. We decide where we want to be in five years, ten years, thirty years down the road, while the lively, restless child within is put in a prison without bars. We also may live with the delusion that we are "in charge" of our lives, that there may not be anything larger to answer to.

From the point of view of Zen practice, it is also necessary to master circumstances, but the way we do it and the final outcome are very different indeed.

> If you become the Master of each circumstance, wherever you stand, whatever you do, is Truth itself.
>
> —*Rinzai*, Rinzai Roku

This quote from the famous modern Zen Master Rinzai is a koan. Implicitly it asks us how to master circumstances, and lets us know that when we do this truly, our life and all our actions become a manifestation of Truth itself.

However, rather than control, plan, and schedule our lives, in Zen we master circumstances simply—by doing zazen. And, when off the cushion, by doing nothing special, just what is needed moment by moment. Instead of being the active "doer," we become witness to the wonder that appears on its own.

> Sitting quietly, doing nothing, spring comes and the grass grows, by itself.
>
> —*Paul Reps*, Zen Telegrams

We do not make the grass grow. This is the height of presumption. It grows by itself.

Doing Nothing

Doing nothing requires vital energy. It does not mean laziness or becoming passive. It means *doing* nothing at all.

A Zen student, Leila, went to the beach for the weekend. After a hectic week she looked forward to peace, to the smell of the ocean, to the sand dunes. There was a woman cleaning in the guest house Leila was staying at. This woman, Frieda, sang very loud love songs in Spanish as she swept the floors. In addition, she was noisy and clumsy.

As usual, Leila woke up early in the morning and wanted to do zazen. She tidied her room, and placed a cushion on the floor to sit on. Just as she sat down on it she heard a bang against the door. Frieda was sweeping outside and had knocked the door with her broom. She was also singing loudly, "My heart's breaking, breaking today."

Leila sat on the cushion, listening to the shrill song.

"What will I do without you?" Frieda kept wailing.

Finally, Leila got up, opened the door and called, "Frieda, can you be a little more quiet?"

Frieda didn't fully understand English and kept right on singing.

Leila went back to sit down again, but not only did the song get louder, the broom started banging her door consistently. Finally, she got up from the cushion wondering what was wrong with the woman. Negative thoughts started to brew, but thanks to years of zazen, she caught herself. "Stop it," she said to the dark mind that was forming. Leila realized that when we want to be apart from something, it clings to us; when we want to be too close, it runs away.

She opened the door and went out of the room. The minute Frieda saw her, she flew over, standing no more than two inches away. It seemed she had taken a great liking to Leila. Leila turned to go outside in the street, and Frieda followed along.

"Where are you going?" she said.

"To the beach," Leila said.

Frieda grinned. "Me too. Going along."

As they walked down the dirt road to the ocean, Frieda kept humming and Leila resisted, trying to shut her out. She started concentrating on other things. Then the humming turned into loud singing again. Leila focused on the delicious salt air and took deep gulps of it. The singing got louder still. Whatever Leila did to block it out, it only got louder. Then, suddenly Master Rinzai's words came to her: "If we master each circumstance, then whatever we do is the truth." *How am I going to master this?* she wondered.

They arrived at the beach with Frieda singing relentlessly. When they got to the sand, Leila spread out a blanket and sat down; Frieda planted herself right beside her again. As Leila watched the waves of the ocean roll up on the shore, she suddenly stopped pushing Frieda away, and fell into zazen. She stopped wanting things to be different. She stopped wanting quiet time alone at the beach. This was the circumstance she was in now, hearing Frieda sing over and over that her heart was breaking.

Suddenly, Leila realized that whoever comes into one's life is none other than one's self. *That's me*, she thought. *My heart must be breaking and Frieda's letting me know. Okay.* She listened to the song carefully. Instead of fighting and pushing it away, she became available to Frieda and her song.

When we *do nothing*, stop trying to fix things, to change things or push them away, they change on their own. First, Leila realized that Frieda was a reflection of her, that everything that comes into our lives is a reflection of ourselves, especially the things we want to push away. She accepted that. *Frieda is me*, she thought, *annoying people, banging, wanting to be too close, with a heart that's breaking*. She hadn't fully realized it before. Now Leila found herself humming along.

Frieda was swaying as she sang, and Leila found herself swaying as well. As the two of them sat there swaying, Frieda's voice became softer. Leila turned and looked at Frieda. Tears were pouring down her face.

Frieda said, "You, my mamma. Missing my mamma."

Leila finally understood that Frieda was missing her mother, who was far away. She must have reminded Frieda of her mother. Frieda was sitting there crying and in a moment Leila started crying as well. She was also missing her mother, who had died a year ago. The two of them sat there crying on the blanket together until Leila turned and gave Frieda a hug. Soon the crying subsided, the singing subsided—they were simply sitting together, listening to the sound of the waves. Circumstance mastered. Moment fulfilled.

There is a saying that each of us carries in our heart enough love to heal this entire planet, but we're so stingy about offering it, we have so much resistance. We prefer to judge, to hate, to push the other way. Perhaps that is why so many of us have to bang at doors, whine, cry, sing too loudly in a voice that is shrill.

Allowing Each Moment to Be As It Is

This story typifies what it means to master circumstances or to do nothing. The situation started to heal and to be mastered the moment Leila allowed Frieda to be who she was and not push her away. Leila had no idea Frieda was so sad and homesick. She also didn't realize how badly she, too, needed to cry. Who is the One who finally knew this, and presented the right action at the right time?

The place we are in will show us how to proceed. We do not have to look anywhere else if we just follow daily life, as it presents itself, and not add anything on. Simple, clear instructions, yet so difficult to follow.

Who Is the Master of Circumstances?

When we practice truthfully, when we do nothing, not only are we with the Master, we become able to spontaneously express what the Master needs and wants. We cry when it's sad, laugh when it's funny, love whatever needs to be loved, and are no longer able to push strangers aside. This is also called *peeling the onion*. It is not theoretical or abstract, just based on what's needed at the time.

As we find the true Master, we realize that although we may never understand what the world is presenting to us, we are still able to be with it, embrace all aspects, and persevere.

> One short pause between the leaky
>   road here,
> And the never-leaking way there,
> If it rains, let it rain.
> If it storms, let it storm.
>
> *—Ikkyu*

No Problem

Life arises as it arises. It is our demand that it turn out differently, that causes our suffering and the suffering we inflict upon others.

We demand that we live forever, never seeing the beauty of aging or older people. We demand that everyone loves us (no matter who), that we make no mistakes, eat only fine food, stay beautiful forever, get what we think is our just due. We go to all lengths to secure these illusions, including putting our true lives at risk. We hide from illness, tragedy, old age and loneliness, abandoning those who are experiencing them. We refuse sorrow and ugliness, not realizing that the ugliness and sorrow are inside of us. Then we wonder why we suffer, trapped in a life without any way out.

The door to escape is through ordinary moments, through persevering in zazen, and through giving attention to all our daily tasks. As we do this, little by little, our ability to bear reality increases, and our suffering subsides. We become of value to others, as we leave nothing uncared for lying around.

> Zen is just picking up your coat from the floor and hanging it up.
> —*Ancient Zen saying*

Not only do we pick up our coats from the floor, but we pick up whatever else is laying there, including people who need to be regarded with respect and love.

ZEN IN ACTION

Exercise 1: Do Nothing

Find a situation that is troubling you and that you have been trying to work out. Think about it and Do Nothing. Think about it again, and Do Nothing again. Stop all unnecessary activity, thoughts, and machinations. Take a walk at the beach (or anywhere that is relaxing to you), enjoy the moment—then think about the situation. Still Do Nothing at all. Keep walking, keep enjoying.

When this situation actually appears in your life, continue to Do Nothing. After about a week of this, notice the changes that have taken place without your interfering at all.

Exercise 2: Find the Master

In the midst of confusion, conflict, and unwanted circumstances, stop and ask yourself, "Where did all this come from? Who is the Master of these circumstances?" Stop and find out now.

Here is a famous quote by the great master Bassui about mastering circumstances:

> When we find the Master, we can rest and do nothing. The Master does all.

PART TWO

CRAVINGS AND COMPULSIONS

CHAPTER 6

QUIETING THE MONKEY MIND

ZEN MIRACLE 6
Our Monkey Mind Dissolves

THE MONKEY MIND

The *Monkey Mind* is the part of ourselves that is constantly restless, jumping from one thing to the next, chattering endlessly, craving, fearing, being unsatisfied, spoiling whatever is at hand. It judges, rejects, lashes out, and is always completely convinced that it, and no one else, is correct. Little by little, it imprisons us in a cage without bars. Life becomes smaller and tighter. When the Monkey Mind gains real power, we cannot eat well, sleep, love, laugh, or find beauty or meaning in life anymore.

LOU'S STORY

Lou, an insomniac, could not sleep more than an hour at a time. He would wake at night in a panic over whether the stock market would go up or down, or if his girlfriend would reject him that day. If the market went up, he felt he was worth something and could keep her love; if it went down, he felt that trouble loomed.

A cold sweat would cover Lou's body as he lay there, imagining life without the love, the money, and the self-esteem he craved. After finally convincing himself that things would be all right, he'd fall back to sleep for an hour or two. Then he'd wake up frantic again, imagining the worst.

When Lou's old school friend Ron called, asking to visit, Lou became even more ill at ease. Though they'd been friends since third grade and he genuinely cared about Ron, Lou couldn't bear to see him again. He was agitated by the way Ron lived. Ron was a writer who wandered about, living in one place and then the next, often staying with friends when his checkbook got low. Unconcerned about his personal finances, Ron usually had a wonderful time, laughing loudly at jokes and feeling tremendously wealthy when a check for an amount such as five thousand dollars came in. He would then immediately plan a trip to a Third World country, where he could live cheaply, enjoy the beautiful scenery, and write until his money ran out.

When Ron called this time, Lou started trembling, and lashed out violently. He accused Ron of being sick, saying that Ron's way of life proved it, and that he didn't want to be around this sickness anymore.

But what is the real sickness here? What is it that is causing Lou such despair, anxiety, and constriction of life? Louis Jourard, author and psychologist, has said that, "We become sick because we act in sickening ways." Although Ron's behavior may have sickened Lou, Lou's own response left much to be desired as well. From a Zen point of view, unbeknownst to Lou, he was simply in the grip of his Monkey Mind.

As we practice Zen, a new part of ourselves emerges and grows strong, bringing freedom from this inner tyrant. We call this new part our *Buddha Nature*. Actually, Buddha Nature is not a new part of ourselves, but something that has been there all along, simply covered by the ignorance and restlessness created by the Monkey Mind. As Buddha Nature emerges, we do not become someone different—we simply reclaim that which we had always been.

The Three Poisons

Where does the Monkey Mind come from? According to Zen, the Monkey Mind is driven and fueled by three poisons—greed, anger, and folly. Unbeknownst to us, most of our lives are driven by these poisons, which we think of as useful qualities. We view greed as strong motivation, and welcome it readily; anger is often seen as self-assertion, a signal of strength. Folly, or ignorance, are the endless delusions that besiege us daily, which are usually taken for truth, and so are acted upon readily. Like a spider, these poisons weave a web that ultimately strangles our lives.

Greed

When in the grip of greed, we search for more and more to satisfy us—*the more the better,* is our mantra. Somehow, what we have is never enough. We live our lives in order to accumulate, store up treasures, hoard them. In this frame of mind, whatever we receive only satisfies momentarily, before we move on to the next. We are like guests at a banquet who eat and eat, but can neither taste the food, nor ever feel full inside.

> We are like a man who, in the midst of water, cries in thirst so imploringly; we are like the son of a rich man who wanders away among the poor.
>
> —*Hakuin Zenji*

As we practice zazen we become able to taste, absorb, and digest both our food and our lives. As we taste and enjoy each bite fully, we need less and less. One bite becomes delicious. It becomes more than enough.

> It was the second morning of week end sesshin (retreat). All day the first day I sat through restlessness, pain, and boredom and wondered what I was doing here. What kept me sitting through

this? When the second morning arrived, I couldn't imagine how I could go on.

We received breakfast seated on our cushions. When the meal server came, I held out my bowl. He placed some oatmeal in it. After everyone was served, we all ate together. I put a little oatmeal in my mouth and shivered. I was stunned, it was so completely delicious. I started to cry. In that moment I realized that no matter how many bowls I had eaten, I had never tasted oatmeal before.

—Zen student

Rather than savor each taste of our lives, we are taught to gulp, to accumulate as much as we can, no matter what the cost, or at whose expense, to cling to our possessions and ultimately feel they are who we are. As we do this, we lose touch with our true needs and basic nature. The further out of touch, the hungrier and more desperate we become, continually seeking more. This is called being a *hungry ghost*. Hungry ghosts feel that in order to make their homes or lives worthwhile and beautiful, they must fill them up, until there is not an empty spot left.

Give Things Away

In Zen practice, we do the opposite. We deeply value empty space. When we want to discover the beauty of our home, we start emptying it out. We take things out and give them away. We clean the house thoroughly. Whatever is inessential is removed. Finally, we have a great deal of empty space. Now we can easily see the home's original beauty. There is nothing extra we need. From the very beginning its value was present. We now also have room to move and breathe. By taking out all unnecessary stuff, we simply uncover our home's original nature. This beauty is intrinsic and cannot be taken away.

We can apply this same process to our hearts and minds. We must clean out, on an ongoing basis, all that which is inessential—

the clutter and accumulations that block our natural beauty and spaciousness. Through zazen this can be accomplished.

When we do not do this, however, when we simply live a life of craving and accumulation, there are many consequences. After the initial happiness of getting what we want, fear arises of losing what we have. We worry that others may become jealous and hate us, or perhaps even steal our treasures away. As we do not know where our real treasure lies, our happiness becomes tinged with anxiety. If our possessions are taken or stolen, if we lose our money, our spouses, our jobs, we feel as though we have lost our value. Many people then live in shame and despair, perhaps even becoming suicidal, feeling they have ultimately failed, and that they are worth nothing.

Others, like Lou, who do not yet know their true nature and value, reject certain people they meet, because these people present aspects of themselves they are terrified of facing. When they are confronted with those in the grip of poverty, illness, or failure, they turn aside. Acts of true kindness become impossible. Is it any wonder that, despite his wealth and investments, Lou cannot sleep at night and is besieged with fear?

The Zen Master and the Robber

An elderly Zen Master was living in a small hut on a mountain, simple and bare except for the few possessions he needed. One night a robber broke into his hut and took everything in it, including the clothes the Zen Master wore on his back.

After the thief left, the Zen Master looked out the window. The moon was shining in. The Zen Master looked at the moon, and sighed.

"Too bad I can't give him this moon too," he said to himself.

This robber could not rob the Zen Master; the Zen Master only wanted to give whatever he had. Beyond that there was nothing the Zen Master had that could be taken away from him. His desire to hold on and accumulate was gone.

THE NATURE OF DESIRE

From a psychological point of view, desires are intrinsic to human life, and we must learn appropriate means of satisfying them. In fact, much psychological illness arises from suppressing and rejecting desire, from unacceptable desires that plague an individual, or from the inability to satisfy deep, persistent longings. Various compensatory mechanisms arise to cope with this, some of which may not be healthy, including symptom formation, fantasy substitution, excessive frustration, poor impulse control, and so forth. Many symptoms are thought to be replacements for the desired object that eludes the individual. In therapy the patient learns how to recognize his desires (conscious and unconscious), accept them, channel them constructively (possibly sublimate some), and receive gratification, which is healthy and positive (as opposed to destructive expression of desire).

This all can be useful and often constructive. Desires are powerful forces and must be recognized and dealt with honestly. A practice that suppresses desire, pretends that it does not exist, or that the individual is beyond human yearning, is based upon an explosive foundation. Sooner or later these unconscious, suppressed energies emerge, often with great harm. It is crucial to recognize the existence of desire, to bring it to awareness, but how we proceed at that point is different in Zen from psychology.

From the Zen view, true gratification never comes from fulfilling desire—temporary relief maybe, but not the deep peace and gratification we seek. As soon as one desire is satisfied, another arises. Satisfaction is fleeting, often leaving the person hungrier than before. Living from desire to desire creates a kind of addiction. We become slaves to our desires—the more we satisfy them, the more we want. At best this is substitute gratification, a counterfeit of the deep peace we are truly longing for.

The state of desirelessness, often described in Buddhist literature, has been misunderstood. It does not mean becoming numb or disconnected. Just the opposite. It means being able to know and fulfill natural and simple needs as they arise without being attached to them, and without craving for more. It separates need and desire. We need a certain amount of food, sunshine, water, friendship. Many desires have nothing to do with our needs, in fact they separate us from them, and create cravings that are unreal.

Again, the saying of Master Rinzai applies:

When I'm hungry I eat, when I'm tired I sleep.
Fools laugh at me, but the wise understand.

EAT WHEN YOU'RE HUNGRY

This simple saying is the basis of all true practice. It restores a person to his or her natural balance and the natural balance of the universe.

How many of us eat when we're hungry, truly tasting and digesting the food we receive? Often, we eat when we're tired, depressed, nervous, or loveless. We eat because it is expected of us socially, or because the time has come to eat. Our needs and compulsions are so mixed up it becomes hard to even know true hunger when it arises. If we eat because we're tired or nervous, we can never be satisfied, and, of course, will always crave more.

How many of us truly sleep when we're tired? How many sleep to block out a painful world, or to escape into dreams? How many can lie down when truly tired, and sleep soundly, not tossing and turning with dreams and fears?

The more we sit, the more we are able to not only know what we truly need, but to satisfy the need directly, before it turns into desire, and we are always begging for more.

An ancient Zen story tells that a woman went to the Buddha and told him she was hungry, starving. She begged him for food. Like most of us, she had become a beggar in life, not realizing where her true nourishment came from. She was willing to eat anything. Whatever was offered by anyone, she grabbed. She looked at the Buddha, her eyes pleading. She was a fish swimming out of water, dying of thirst.

The Buddha held out food to her, but would not let her have it. First she had to say "no" to him. She had to realize she wasn't a beggar. She had to put a stop to greed.

Having It All

We go through life, to lovers, friends, therapists, as beggars, pleading for an end to our suffering. When faced with anxiety and anguish, much of present-day treatment deals with it either by giving medication to numb the pain, or utilizing techniques so that an individual can get what he's craving, become wealthy, *have it all.* This is like giving the starving woman food that will not fill her up, but make her more hungry.

Rather than view greed as a positive factor and allow it to drive us, the first step is to see it for what it is and realize its consequences. No matter how much money Lou accumulates, he will never feel safe or satisfied. In fact, the more he gives into this craving, the less fulfilled he will feel and the more desperate he will become.

Modern-day treatment rarely questions the fundamental nature of success or identity. Achievement and accumulation are encouraged, no matter what lack they serve to compensate for. The question of who we are fundamentally, before achievement and accumulation, is not looked into. Many fall into despair after their goals have been realized, after they "got" all they wanted, and still feel the deep emptiness within. *Is this all there is?* they wonder. This is especially prevalent during the time of retirement because up to then an individual's sense of identity and worth had been based upon his or her work, or the income it provided.

Psychology is struck dumb when it hears the Zen injunction:

Gain and Loss, Away With Them, Once and For All.
　　　　　　　　　　　　　　—*Sosan*, On Believing In Mind

Nothing to Be Gained, Nothing to Be Lost

A Sutra is a teaching of the Buddha. The Heart Sutra, one basic Zen text, tells us, "There is nothing to be gained, nothing to be lost. This Sutra puts an end to all suffering. This is the truth, not a lie."

This Sutra is a fundamental teaching of the Buddha about the nature of life itself. It speaks of the phenomenal world (the world of form), the absolute (the world of emptiness), and suffering (the world of human beings). The Sutra teaches that all form turns into emptiness and all emptiness into form; it is our clinging to one or the other, our delusion that they are permanent, that creates suffering. It is the delusion that there is something to be gained, that we must not lose it, which strikes fear in our hearts. This Sutra tells us to look beyond that, where we cannot lose anything.

When we understand this and stop clinging, the Monkey Mind starts to dissolve and suffering comes to an end.

The Nature of Suffering

In order to put an end to suffering, it is necessary to understand what truly causes it. We must look at the arising of the three poisons, and how not to get caught. Then we must *do* it. Understanding is not enough.

The Wheel of Karma

According to Zen, human life, in its conditioned (or unawakened) form, is run by "karma"—an endless chain of cause and effect, reaching back through time, composed of our thoughts, words, and deeds. This idea is present in Western thought as well, "*As we sow, so shall we reap.*" That which we think, say, or do has consequences that extend into time. When we meet with certain conditions, these consequences ripen, and the effects blossom in our lives. Sooner or later, all seeds we have planted yield their fruit—bitter seeds, bitter fruit, sweet seeds, sweet fruit. The process is continuous.

For example, greed forces us to take and take, but what do we give in return? How are the scales balanced? Sooner or later we must receive in our lives exactly what we have given. All debts require payment; we must give back what has been given to us. When this process is deeply understood, one's life can be redirected.

The endless chain of circumstances we become caught in, our persistent dreams, longings, struggles, fears, are all a reflection of this. In Freudian psychology this is called the repetition compulsion, where we unconsciously and compulsively repeat the same situation in our lives over and over. It is usually a traumatic situation that we are seeking to master, in order to make it turn out differently (which it seldom does). The wheel of karma keeps turning.

In Zen practice, rather than trying to make a situation turn out differently, we "master" it by knowing what it truly is—a persistent dream or delusion. We undo the power it has over us by becoming aware of its essential nature, and by not reacting. This nonreaction, or nonmoving, is a way of ending the karma, taking back the energy we have given to the situation, making it less and less real. As we refuse to live our lives based upon the three poisons, the fuel or fire that keeps the wheel turning is slowly put out.

Our nonreaction, or nonmoving, means that we do not react to the endless chain of thoughts, wishes, temptations, and desires that besiege us daily, both within and without. In this way we are putting an end to the karma of constant automatic reactions, and take a step off the merry-go-round of life, and onto solid ground.

> I ask this wanting creature inside me,
> What is the river you want to cross?
> —*Kabir*

ACCEPTING ALL PARTS OF OURSELVES

In Zen practice we do not label an experience "good" or "bad." This only makes it more solid. We never accept one part and throw the other away. Zen practice is about becoming whole. Both Lou and Ron are parts of the fabric of ourselves. One is not better than the other. Both parts of ourselves need to be met and known.

According to Zen we all have, or are, Buddha Nature. This means we are all originally joyful, loving, and clear. Despite the karma we live with, there is not anything fundamentally wrong with us. We do not need any medicine. How did we become beggars then, swimming in the water while dying of thirst? What has happened to our Buddha Nature? Where did it go?

Nowhere. It is completely present day by day. It is only the poisons and afflictions we carry that cover it like thunderclouds. Practice brushes the clouds away. Our fear, anxiety, dread, and greed operate only upon the surface of our lives. As we go deeper into quiet waters, our real nature soon emerges.

In order to allow this true nature to emerge what we do is to stop reacting and start understanding what kind of craving or desire we are dealing with, whether it is constructive and can ever give us what we truly want. The stopping is crucial. It quiets the turbulent mind and heart.

WHEN CHAOS ARISES

When greed arises, we become aware that greed has appeared. Instead of allowing it to run rampant, we stop and experience the feeling of wanting more and more, the pain of being unable to be satisfied. Rather than tossing about in waves of frustration and allowing it to dictate chaotic actions, we simply experience our frustration deeply. As we do this, we realize the true nature of our entire lives.

Doing Nothing is one of the greatest antidotes for chaos, for the Monkey Mind which, by its very nature, loves to struggle and solve challenges. Doing Nothing is the Monkey Mind's greatest terror. It prefers to become busier and busier, entangled in all sorts of complications. The busier, the better, it warns us—the more we do, the more alive we will become. This lie leads to all kinds of madness and suffering.

We cannot stop the noise outside, but we can stop ourselves.

—Trungpa

True action, which arises from nondoing, comes when the Monkey Mind is stilled. True action is the ability to be present, to see, hear, and to respond to the real world. True action allows us to respond, not react. It lets a long breath be long and a short breath be short. It allows events to speak to us, instead of imposing our will and interpretation upon them. Nondoing is vital and powerful. It harnesses our vagrant energies and causes us to become strong. It requires patience and trust.

> Do you have the patience to wait
> Till your mind settles
> And the water is clear?
> Can you remain unmoving
> Till the right
> Action comes by itself?
> *—the Buddha*, Dhammpada

As the Monkey Mind is eliminated all kinds of other riches appear. This is exemplified in the story of Cara, a Zen student on Long Island who was selling an old colonial house she had lived in for years with her large family.

THE RICHEST WOMAN IN TOWN

Because so many children lived in Cara's house, and so many friends came to visit, she kept it simple, rather bare inside. There were cushions scattered everywhere to sit on, bamboo furniture, plants, paintings. The most striking part of the house was that most of the outside walls had been turned into windows so that light could pour in, and the trees and grass be easily seen. There were skylights in almost every room and Cara was happy with her home and the endless guests who enjoyed it as well.

When the house went on the market many buyers passed through. They looked around disgruntled, not finding what they were looking for. There were no crystal chandeliers; the kitchen was large, with a round, wooden table and fresh herbs growing, but it had not been renovated for many years. The bathrooms were charming, as they had been originally, with nothing new added. Most people enjoyed the walk through, but left without returning. For months no one made a bid.

Finally, an agent called, telling Cara that she was bringing a "hot prospect." This man was desperate to move quickly. He had plenty of money and liked the location. Cara had better spruce the house up as much as possible. Things looked good.

A man arrived in a Cadillac, dressed in a dark, silk suit with a large diamond ring on his pinky. He walked up to the front door as though the house were already his. Cara welcomed him in, but he didn't pause a moment, just confidently glided through the rooms. She stood back and watched. Soon he began stomping from one room to another, then, puzzled, he returned and stopped in front of her.

"You call this a home?" he said, unbelievingly.

"Of course," Cara said.

"For you, maybe," he grimaced, "but look at me. I'm wealthy. I have important friends. I entertain lavishly. Do you know how much work this place needs?"

"None at all," said Cara.

He took a step closer. Dead silence. Then he said, "Didn't you hear me? I'm a wealthy man."

"Not as wealthy as I am. Haven't they told you?" Cara smiled slowly. "I'm the richest woman in town."

His eyes went blank as he stared at her.

"When it rains I can hear the rain on the windows," she said, "and when the sun shines I can feel the sun. The trees and sky outside are always with me."

The man turned and left as fast as he could.

ZEN IN ACTION

Exercise 1: Greeting the Hungry Ghost

Ask yourself what it is you are truly wanting, that you think temporary acquisitions fulfill? Who is the hungry ghost inside you? Where does he live? Do not reject him. Become familiar with that part of yourself.

Exercise 2: "This Suffices"

When frustration and restlessness arise, ask: *What am I wanting now? What is wrong with what I have?* Be completely where you are at this moment, and with what you have at present. We rarely experience what is before us now, as we start wanting something more or better, something that will make our lives seem worthwhile.

A wonderful remedy for persistent restlessness is to say, "This suffices." This is from a Tibetan teaching offered by Tulku Thondup. Whatever is given to you, look at it and say, "This suffices." This is a practice of welcoming all that life offers. It is a way of calming the ravenous being inside us that refuses to accept what is given and be satisfied. Another way of saying this is, "Thy will be done." Or, "Thank you."

Exercise 3: Meeting Our Cravings Face to Face

Take a moment and consider what the cravings and compulsions are in your life. What do you feel you cannot live without? What kind of price do you pay for it? What kind of fulfillment does this craving provide? Just look at these questions. Mull them over gently. Live with them from day to day. Your responses may change from moment to moment. Let them.

Allow change to happen. It will anyway.

Developing a Grateful Mind

Developing a grateful mind is a wonderful antidote to insatiable hunger. We rarely realize or appreciate all that is constantly being given to us, moment by moment. Instead of focusing upon what they are being given, most spend their time focusing upon what they do not have, or how to exchange the gifts they receive. It is this mind itself that turns us into beggars.

There is a wonderful exercise called *Naikan*, developed in Japan, geared to addressing this issue. It works to break our focus upon all that we lack, and put our attention instead on what we are receiving. This exercise is truly Zen in motion, in everyday life.

Exercise 4: Naikan

Spend about thirty to forty minutes a day with this exercise. (There are also Naikan retreats available, where it can be done all day long.)

Make a careful, specific list of all you have received today. Be careful not to overlook small things. Everything matters.

Make another list of all you have given. (Usually we think we are giving all day long and receiving very little. This list will surprise you. Don't leave anything out.)

Now make a third list of any trouble or pain you may have caused anybody. Some think this list will induce guilt. It may or it may not. The purpose of the list is simply to reverse our usual thinking, where we feel hurt and disappointed by others most of the time, and do not look at what trouble or pain we may have caused.

For the purposes of this chapter, we will focus upon the first list. All three are naturally interconnected and work beautifully together. (You can also do Naikan on a person and relationship. This will be discussed in a future chapter.)

Zen is the practice of sincerity. Saying "thank you" with a full mind and heart is enlightenment itself.

Our insatiable Monkey Mind cannot slow down and diminish until we learn how to receive. As we sit silently on the cushion, we do this. We receive our breath. Who gave it? Where would we be without it? Where does it come from? Where does it go? What must we do to deserve it? Nothing. This breath is purely given, and purely used.

Did you receive breakfast this morning? Lunch? Did someone call to say hello? Did you receive the rays of the sun as it was shining, or the smile of a woman who passed you on the street? Were you there to receive it? Were you willing to do so? Did you take a moment to stop and speak to her? What else did you give in return? To whom?

Many of us must learn what it means to receive. We block the gifts sent to us, do not say "thank you" for them. We may feel they are our due, or that they are not good enough, that we deserve more and better. Rather than feel grateful, we may be fuming inside.

As we sit on the cushion to practice, it is impossible not to realize all that we are receiving, and to welcome it with open hands.

CASE 27: (FROM *HEKIGANROKU*— TRANSLATED AS *THE BLUE CLIFF RECORDS*)

Ummon was a great Zen Master of the late T'ang, who died in 949. Like Rinzai he used vigorous language and shocking tactics to help his students wake up.

Koan: Ummon's Golden Breeze

A monk asked Ummon, "What will happen when trees wither and leaves fall?"

Ummon said, "You embody the golden breeze."

SETCHO'S VERSE

> Significant the question,
> Pregnant the answer, too!
> The three phrases are satisfied,
> The arrow penetrates the universe.
> The wind blows across the plain,
> Soft rain clouds the sky.

As the Monkey Mind disappears, the golden breeze blows and blows.

CHAPTER 7

LONELINESS AND SEPARATION

ZEN MIRACLE 7
We finally meet the Friend.

Remember there's only one
reason to do anything;
A meeting with the Friend
is the only real payment.
            —*Kabir*

The greatest pain we all bear is the pain of separation, of loneliness, of feeling unwanted and forgotten in an impersonal universe. Much of our lives revolve around the endless struggle not to experience this. We tell ourselves that we matter, that love is available, that there are an abundance of friends and lovers waiting for us out there. We go to parties, fall in love, marry, have children, colleagues, business associates, all in an attempt to have the experience of having love and support.

When a relationship ends, or if one is having difficulty finding or keeping a love partner, gnawing doubts and fears start to emerge. Questions arise, such as, *Am I worth loving? Is there some-*

thing wrong with me? What can I do to make myself more loveable, more attractive to the opposite sex? There is very little a person will not do to assure himself and others that indeed he is a significant person, loved, cared for and admired, that he has not failed at this most precious quest in life—that of being loved.

The Craving to Be Loved

Most relationships are based upon the craving to be loved. Not to be loving, but to be loved—to have one's ego and sense of self-importance affirmed. This is a quest for approval and validation in the eyes of another, and no matter how much we receive, usually it is never enough. The more we receive, the deeper the craving grows.

For many the experience of need, dependence, possessiveness, incompleteness, or control are thought to be love. The desire or craving for another person and the intense feelings it can generate are the basis for many relationships. It is easy to see that these feelings are not based in love, as the individuals caught in these webs begin to battle for power, control, or constant affirmation, as love turns to hate and then rejection.

From the Zen point of view, this kind of love is a trap. Even when we think we have it, the hungry heart is still not full. An important core of Zen practice is to dislodge us from addiction to counterfeit forms of love.

Most feel they have lost something precious in their lives. They have no idea where it has gone or how to retrieve it. Many believe they will find it when they find that one special person or relationship that will take their loneliness away and fill their hungry hearts. But a temporary respite from loneliness cannot give them what they truly crave. Even if the relationship lasts for many years, sooner or later they must be alone with themselves. The further they search for love outside themselves, and the more they think they've found it, the deeper essential loneliness can grow.

Searching for the Soul Mate

Theodore sought his soul mate relentlessly. After corresponding with a woman in Europe for quite some time he decided that she was the one, and planned a trip to meet her.

"Soon I will actually see her," he told his therapist before he left.

When he returned from the trip, he went to see the therapist again.

"I was right," he told her. "She was my soul mate and I asked her to marry me on the second date. I thought time was short and I'd better let her know how I felt. She turned me down."

The therapist asked him, "What would you have done if she had said yes?"

He said, "I would have had my hands full. But I know that once I have that soul mate, hands full or not, everything will be beautiful."

This is a fine example of love as a mirage, or a placebo. After going to many different therapists, Theodore finally embarked upon the practice of Zen. His therapists had labeled him neurotic. His Zen Master told him to just "sit." From a Zen point of view, labeling him neurotic is a judgment, which diminishes possibilities for him; it implants in him an identity that may be hard to escape. When he tells his Zen Master he is relentlessly seeking his soul mate, his Zen Master smiles. "Keep sitting and you will find it." Of course, what he expects Theodore to find is something different from what Theodore is expecting.

> The musk is inside the deer,
> But the deer does not look for it,
> It wanders around looking for grass.
> —*Kabir*

From the Zen view, a soul mate is not someone outside of yourself. It's not an object you find that will make you whole magically. The longing for a soul mate is not ultimately for a person, but a longing to end the suffering and separation an individual feels. So, in Zen practice we learn how to end the suffering. As we do this we find that everyone may be our soul mate—or that we're with our soul mate right now. We may even greet our soul mate when we see the sun shine through the window or the children playing on the streets.

This is not a rejection of human relationships, but when love is turned into a substance to provide security or end suffering, this kind of love is considered counterfeit. When we think we're going to have a perfect situation with any person, inevitably, we will be disappointed and hurt. Life and relationships are about one thing only: change, change, change.

As many people live lonely lives, searching for love or desperately trying to cling to what they've found, they become hopeless about ever finding fulfillment. No matter how many people they know, or relationships they have been in, as time passes and change happens they feel fundamentally alone.

Something Is Always Missing

"Something is always missing," Karla said. "In the beginning of the relationship I never realize it, or suspect it's going to turn out this way again. He always seems like the perfect one, finally. We're happy, excited, deeply in love, and then—reality sets in. Little traits of his start to annoy me. He forgets to call when he says he will. I start wondering who he really is. He starts looking at me critically, too. Our time together becomes run-of-the-mill, and the thrill of seeing him disappears. I can always tell the moment it's over. I look at him and wonder what I loved. Suddenly he's a stranger, and I'm a stranger to myself as well. I don't feel beautiful anymore. The light has gone from my eyes."

Of course, the light can never leave Karla, but her experience indicates that something vital has disappeared. She was living in the grip of counterfeit love, the mirage of love, responding to an illusion. Karla initially saw her boyfriend as perfect. She most likely knew very little about him. Was she ever able to actually see, taste, or touch him? Did she see the part of him that is perfect, no matter what? Did she realize his Buddha Nature?

FALLING IN LOVE WITH OUR FANTASIES

What Karla loved was her fantasy about her boyfriend, not him. All fantasies fade; they have to—that is the nature of dreams. In the beginning the fantasy felt wonderful, though, and the beauty of it reflected upon her. She must also be perfect, she thought, if someone like him could love her. Then reality sets in.

To Karla, only fantasy, not reality, could ever be perfect. Reality was an enemy. Daily life is an opponent of fantasy; it always forces us to be who we are and see what is before us, whether we like it or not. Karla did not like reality, and blamed it on her boyfriend, not on her own unwillingness to be with life as it is. Instead she felt it was he who was deficient, and that she would find someone beautiful somewhere else.

Similarly, a young Zen student was extremely shocked and dismayed when she learned things about a senior student she had not known before. In a state of anxiety, she went to another student.

"I loved him so much," she said. "I thought he was so beautiful, so perfect, such an example of Zen. Now my dreams are smashed."

The friend looked at her slowly. "You didn't love him at all," he said. "You loved your fantasies about him. If you can know the whole truth, and still love him, then that is really love."

Karla was also unable to love the truth of life, to see the real beauty surrounding her. As long as we do not know what love is, do not know how to receive another person, the hungry heart can never fill up.

> Kabir says this—just throw away all thoughts
> of imaginary things
> and stand firm in that which you are.

Throw Away Thoughts of Imaginary Things

We have little idea how to throw away imaginary thoughts and false expectations. When we give to others we expect to have our gifts returned, expect others to behave in certain ways. When these expectations are not met, the relationship immediately takes a different turn. If this happens frequently, the so-called love we have been feeling turns to hate, resentment, or the bitter taste of feeling we have been made a fool. Living in this manner, it will surely be difficult to meet the Friend (to have a real encounter with love).

When this pattern repeats too many times, some become unable to be in a relationship and instead live behind a wall, trying to protect themselves from failure and pain. Some insist that relationships are just too painful. They've had their fill, feel relationships only create more loneliness than before. These individuals may not be aware of the deeper problem—that they are not truly in a relationship at all, but are caught in the grip of counterfeit love. Like most mirages, counterfeit love grabs its unsuspecting victims and leaves them emptier than before. Zen practice comes to cure this, showing us how to dissolve all mirages.

From the psychological point of view healthy defenses are necessary. It is important to know who to love and who to reject. It is important to discriminate between individuals, casting away some and receiving others. While this gives us the sense of greater control of ourselves and our world, there is a price we pay for this as well. The price of not being all that we truly are.

From the Zen point of view, while discrimination is important, when our true selves are found, when real love (as opposed to attachment and mirages) is experienced, no one need ever be rejected, including ourselves.

> Wherever we go we recreate our shells (hells), like an insect carrying its shell on its body. We feel our shell keeps us safe, but it crushes us and others, and keeps out light and sun.
>
> —*Zen Master Taisen Deshimaru*

COUNTERFEIT LOVE

Let us stop for a moment and look more deeply at counterfeit love, the source of true pain in relationships. Counterfeit love includes the idea that love is a feeling, not a way of life. It is confusion between excitement, dependence, attachment, possession, and the experience of love. In real love there is no rejection or sense of separation from another or from ourselves. Before we become able to be this way with another, we must be able to be this way with ourselves.

In counterfeit love, when we have strong feelings toward someone, we immediately declare that we are in love. As all feelings change and pass into new feelings, most people are convinced that love cannot last. When their loving feelings turn unpleasant, they blame it upon the other and find all kinds of things wrong with them. Eventually that person is discarded.

Real love never discards anybody; it knows and accepts transience, never tries to hold the other back.

Psychologically speaking, we are trained to make sure that we are treated by others with consideration and respect. If this is not forthcoming, we consider it bad for our sense of self worth and are taught to leave the person behind and find someone new. In this model, our health becomes tied to the behavior of others. Our disposable society includes human beings, even those we have once dearly loved.

"I say good-bye after the third date if they don't meet my needs," Tim said proudly, "and I don't just mean my needs in the bedroom—I mean my needs every place." Tim is a vital guy in his thirties who is looking for love in his life. "I'm a great catch," he says loudly, "anyone will be lucky to get me. I know what I want and if I get it, I'll give a lot back in return."

What Tim can't understand is why he's so lonely and unable to find that right person for him. Of course no one will ever be the right person for Tim until he himself becomes right.

Tim and others like him do not realize that their way of being turns people into objects, used to fulfill their personal needs. The crucial word for Tim is *if*. If he gets what he wants, he'll give it as well. He'll stroke your ego *if* you stroke his in return. This is not true giving, but barter, like in the marketplace. The relationship becomes a commodity. You play your role and he'll play his. Tim wants someone he can wear on his arm to walk down the street in order to be admired. He never stops to ask, "Admired for what? By whom?"

When we turn another person into an object, we never know who it is before us right now. We miss the incredible opportunity for the communion and connection we so desperately long for. We kill the other's inwardness, and in the same stroke kill ourselves as well.

> When you really look for me,
> you will see me instantly.
>
> —*Kabir*

ZEN IN ACTION

Exercise 1: Surrendering Expectations

Make a list of what it is you expect in relationships, what you feel you can't live without. Now, make another list of relationships you have had, which have been just fine without expectations. In your present relationship, consciously give up one expectation a day. Let the relationship be just as it is. See how you and your partner feel.

Exercise 2: The Craving to Love

List all of the people you want to be loved by, and what you have done to make this happen. Write down the result. Have you been more loved? What else have you tried then? Now, turn it all around. Each day give that person exactly what you have wanted to receive. Do it mindfully, not overstepping boundaries. How do you feel now? What is happening to the relationship?

Exercise 3: Unmasking Counterfeit Love

Describe what love means to you. Describe some situations in which you felt this was it, only to be horribly disappointed. Where did you go wrong? What did you take to be love that might have merely been infatuation, need, dependence, attachment, fear, etc. Look at this carefully. Begin to see what love is differently. Keep a diary about this. You'll be amazed.

CASE 12: (FROM *MUMONKAN—* TRANSLATED AS *THE GATELESS GATE*)

Koan: Zuigan Calls Himself "Master"

THE CASE

Zuigan Gen Osho called to himself every day, "Master!" and answered, "Yes, sir!" Then he would say, "Be wide awake!" and answer, "Yes, sir!" "Henceforward, do not be deceived by others!" "No, I won't."

MUMON'S COMMENTARY

"Old Zuigan himself buys and sells himself. He takes out a lot of God-masks and devil-masks and puts them on and plays with them. What for? One calling and the other answering; one wide awake, the other saying he will never be deceived. If you stick to any of them, you will be a failure. If you imitate Zuigan, you will play the fox."

MUMON'S VERSE

Clinging to the deluded way of consciousness,
Students of the Way do not realize truth.
The seed of birth and death through endless eons:
The fool calls it the true original self.

There are many elements in this wonderful koan. But let us look at one of them here. Who is calling? Who is answering? Who is it that is deceived by others? It looks like one person is talking to himself. Can that be so?

Look carefully for yourself and see who it is you speak to; see who it is that is deceived by others. Then you will never be deceived again.

CHAPTER 8

FEEDING THE HUNGRY HEART

ZEN MIRACLE 8
We stop rejecting others and ourselves.

Rejection is one of the most painful experiences in relationships—not only rejection from others, but our rejection of ourselves. Many of our defenses and interpersonal manipulations are created to avoid this blow to our sense of worth. In psychology, much time is spent dealing with this, unraveling the ways in which as children we have taken in negative messages about ourselves and turned them into who we are now. We also notice the way in which our rejection of our parents (or their rejection of us), is projected by us onto our entire world. In order to avoid the experience of being rejected, many reject others first. This ensures them of being the one in power, not crushed and left behind.

However, Zen practice has a different take on this. As we practice we see that our entire lives are built upon the activity of rejection. From the moment we wake up in the morning until we go to sleep, we are busy rejecting what life has to offer. We are constantly accepting some experiences and throwing away many others. Indeed, rejection can be thought of as "the disease of the mind."

To separate what we like from what we dislike is the disease of
the mind.

—*Sosan*, On Believing in Mind

Separating What We Like
from What We Dislike

This famous quote suggests that the pain and loss we experience
in relationships has nothing to do with the other person, it is a
disease lodged within our own mind. We cause this suffering by
separating what we like from what we dislike, by constantly judg-
ing and condemning others, by refusing our love if a person
doesn't make the grade.

To separate what we like from what we dislike kills all relationships both with others and with ourselves. This basic tenet of
Zen is a profound instruction both for meditation and relationships in everyday life.

We love one and hate another, we choose him and reject her.
We admire the rich and step over the homeless. We look up at
the masters, and down at beginning students. We sit in judgment
upon all of life, never stopping to ask ourselves, Who are we to
judge anyone? Who made us judge and jury? Can we truly be so
arrogant to judge and reject this immense world that has been
given to us to love? Has it been given to us to dispose of it harshly?
Or has it been given to tend? In order to feed our hearts, which
are always so hungry, we must turn this usual way of behaving
around one hundred and eighty degrees. This is an everyday life
koan that should be dwelt upon daily.

When we meet with someone noisy, rude or unpleasant, this
is a wonderful opportunity. Rather than push the person aside, it
is the perfect time to practice—do not separate what you like from
what you dislike. Accept that person and be with him fully, just as
he is. Become aware if you are sitting in judgment, and if so, stop
it. Reject your own negative thoughts—do not reject others.

Do Not Look for the Faults of Others

> Do not look for the faults of others,
> Look at your own deeds
> Done and undone.
> —*the Buddha*, Dhammapada

If we feel there is something wrong with everyone we meet, that we have to fix, change, or instruct them, it is wise to listen more deeply to the Buddha's teachings on relationships.

> Do not seek to straighten another
> Do a harder thing instead—
> Straighten yourself.

This is a vitally different orientation from what we are used to. Here we see that loneliness is not our intrinsic nature, that it arises from selfishness, from projecting our faults onto others or trying to control and change them. In fact, Shantideva goes even a step further in *The Bodhisattva's Way of Life*. Rather than find ways to get back at others or feel like a victim, this is what he recommends when someone has greatly hurt or disappointed you:

> When someone whom I have helped
> or in whom I have placed great hope
> harms me with great injustice,
> may I see that one as a sacred friend.
> —*Shantideva*

This person is a great, sacred friend because he has come into our lives to teach us patience, endurance, compassion, to purify us of negative karma or poisons that we have accumulated over long periods of time. Based upon our earlier discussion of cause and effect, we understood that this painful event would not be now happening to us, if we had not set certain causes into effect at one time or another. Nothing is random or purposeless.

Understanding this, we stand up tall, accept what is happening and take responsibility for our part in how we perceive oth-

ers, respond to them, and interact with them. As we do this, it is
easy to see that our isolation and loneliness comes from our endless rejection, judgment and hatred of others (and in the same
manner, also of ourselves). Of course we will feel lonely and iso-
lated when we live in this way. Perhaps we deserve to. When we
open our arms and our heart to the whole world and are willing
to meet it just as it is, the whole world opens its whole arms to us
as well. More important, we see there is nothing to reject, we are
all one.

> Open your hands,
> If you want to be held.
> —*Rumi*

Making Acquaintance with All That Is

The experience of acceptance and oneness is a basic fruit of Zen
practice. As we sit without moving, without escaping and running
away, we are forced to make acquaintance with all that is within
us. Like it or not, we cannot separate that which we dislike from
that which we like. We must see, feel, and taste whatever thoughts,
memories, and feelings come to mind. We cannot escape ourselves
on the cushion. As we sit more deeply, we learn that the pain we
experience in our zazen comes from rejecting and fighting unwanted
parts of ourselves. As we stop fighting and rejecting, an amazing
thing happens: no matter what comes, we feel joy, realizing we are
all one.

One Life

This experience of nonresisting dissolves our walls of alienation
and reminds us that we are all fundamentally united, fellow travelers upon this vast earth. Whoever appears before us is simply
another face of ourselves, a different possibility. Why have we

been resisting them? Zen says that all have been our mothers and fathers at one time or another. They have all tried their best for us. Rejection is not necessary. Curiosity is a better response.

Whether we want to do this or not, life itself will help us. Life is wonderful practice for making this teaching our flesh and bones. Just stop looking for what is wrong with the other and what is right with us. Stop looking out for number one. In fact, number one includes everyone.

As this happens we naturally develop Big Mind, or Parental Mind—the mind that accepts, does not cling, nurtures, heals, and upholds all of life. Dogen Zenji, a great Zen Master, gives us a wonderful description of someone who has attained this condition:

> When he was completely enlightened he could walk through mud and be splashed with dirty water without being upset. He simply accepted mud as mud—and dirty water as water. He was a free man, unattached to ideas of like or dislike. Such power comes from nonattachment.

PARENTAL MIND

In order to develop Parental Mind, we must take ultimate responsibility for everything that appears in our lives. We don't choose one thing and reject another—the homeless man on the street is just as precious as our own child. Though this attitude may seem impossible in the beginning, with time, patience, and steady practice, this kind of mind naturally grows.

From the psychological point of view we frequently work on the client's primal relationship with the mother. This is complicated because many people have a so-called love-hate relationship with their mothers. There is the bad mother who we do not like and the good mother we are always longing for. As we grow older we turn certain individuals (male and female), in our lives into the bad mother, and others into the good mother, thus split-

ting and separating everything. We develop a strong image of how
the good mother is supposed to behave. As soon as the person
deviates from that, he or she becomes the bad mother, and seems
to deserve our rage. There are countless ways we find to punish
them for our disappointment.

As we grow up, we still harbor that desire and fantasy. Not
only do we want the good mother to act a certain way, but to forever provide us with unconditional love. As a baby we didn't have
to earn love, and even though we are older now many of us still
demand that unconditional response, no matter how we behave.
Of course, as we grow older we don't get the unconditional
response. We may not have even gotten it with our mothers when
we were young. This can then become justification, once again,
for our anger, disappointment, and rejection in relationships.

But human love and human relationships naturally fluctuate.
They are happy, unhappy, sad, close, distant, trustworthy, and full
of games. Sometimes we love someone very much, and then when
he or she does something we don't like, the love is suddenly gone,
dislike grows, apprehension grows, and before long he or she may
seem like an enemy. Our task in this practice, however, is to develop
the true nature of friendship, of kindness, of unconditional regard.

Sweet Mamma, Be Kind to Me

A Zen student was asked to teach a class on Zen meditation in a
learning center in Times Square. Of course, usually when we go
to do zazen we think of going to a beautiful place where all is clean
and quiet. The place was right near the train station in a noisy,
dirty room. She came with a bell and a pack of incense. A bunch
of big, tough people sauntered into the room, people who seemed
to have no idea what Zen was. She told them all to sit down on
the floor, cross their legs, and straighten their backs. There wasn't
much time for the class and she wanted to get to the heart of the
matter. So these people sat down on the floor, straightened their
backs, and began to look more lively and beautiful.

She explained how to do zazen, rang the bell, and they all began.

They were sitting a short time when one yelled out, "Oh sweet mamma, be kind to me. Let me move."

She looked at the clock. They'd only been sitting five minutes. "Don't move," she replied.

In another two minutes, he called out again, "Pain! I'm in pain!"

She didn't answer and didn't move.

"Sweet mamma," he called more loudly still, "did you hear me? I'm in pain!"

When we're in pain we call for our mamma. He was basically begging, "Be kind. Let me move."

On the surface it looked as though she was being cruel by not allowing him relief, wanting him to feel his pain.

He kept calling, "Mamma, mia. Be kind."

From our human point of view, being kind involves taking away pain, giving a piece of chocolate candy, comforting. We confuse love and comfort. We want tons of comfort. When someone we love seems to cause us pain, they are not a "good mamma" anymore.

There is a different kind of comfort in Zen practice. As we sit more and more we receive deep comfort, but not from being allowed to move or escape our pain, not from running away. Whatever comes to us on cushion—great joy, great trouble, pain, delight—our comfort comes in accepting it all. Being kind means learning how to accept all of our experiences and allowing them to transform, because they do not transform themselves when we run away.

In this practice we have two officers in the zendo—the *jiki-jitsu* who plays the role of a strict father, who yells, "Sit. Don't move. Stop whining. Hold your back straight." Then we have the *jisha*, who plays the role of mamma, brings tea, cares for us. Both are needed. In the zendo, mother is precious, but mother isn't always soft. And beyond that, we must learn where mother really is, who mother really is, how to become our own mother.

But how do we become our own mother? Is it possible? Absolutely. Not only possible, but necessary. Because the human world, and psychological interaction is always full of good mother/bad mother, I love you/I don't love you, I want you/I hate you, come closer/get away. With one hand we pull, with another we push. Even within ourselves we devise the good and bad mother. But to become our own mother we must sit through it all.

When Great Love Grows

When great love grows we become the mother, not only for ourselves, but everyone else. The mind that doesn't discriminate is the mother, it is great love. It is the mind inside of ourselves that isn't blaming, choosing, hating, that is the mother within us.

Great love is real love. Great love can't be affected by external conditions. We can also call it great compassion, or oneness with all beings, our own true nature. This can only grow by really knowing who we are, finding the real source of mothering. And when great love begins to grow we can give it to all people without thinking, *This one is good, this one is bad, I love you, I hate you.* In fact the person does not ever have to earn our love, they deserve it just because there they are.

> Are you looking for me? I am in the
> next seat.
> My shoulder is against yours.
> You will not find me in stupas, not in
> Indian shrine
> Rooms, nor in synagogues, nor in
> cathedrals:
> Not in masses, nor kirtans, not in legs
> winding
> Around your own neck, nor in eating
> nothing but
> Vegetables.
>
> —*Kabir*

The Zen Master and His Nephew

There is a wonderful story about a great Zen Master who was called by his brother and asked to come home and help with his nephew. The boy had become a rebel, staying out late at night, smoking, drinking, and making trouble. No matter how hard others tried to change and help him, he would listen to no one. His behavior grew worse daily, and the family was frightened.

The Zen Master agreed to visit for one week. He arrived at his brother's home and just went along with the daily routine, spoke pleasantly to the nephew about this and that, never mentioning his behavior. The nephew kept on waiting for his uncle to reprimand him. Instead the Master accompanied his nephew on his trips here and there. They spent time together, and still the Master said nothing.

Finally, the week passed and the time came for the Master to go home. The nephew stood close by, waiting for the scolding. Instead, as the Master bent over to tie his shoes, he began to silently cry. The nephew saw teardrops rolling down the Master's cheeks and was deeply shaken. He could not move or say a word. From that time on, his behavior changed. He could not act the old way, even if he wanted to.

The Master lived in Parental Mind, where all beings were accepted. He did not live in a world of blame. He had no need to judge, reject, or scold his nephew. Feeling so accepted and loved, the nephew could not help but open himself to another way of life.

Zen in Action

*Exercise: 1: Never Give Up on a Person—
Never Give Up on Yourself*

Here is an instruction to use in everyday life and is a remedy for the poisonous ways we have been in relationships. It comes from

Lojong. (*Lojong* are part of Tibetan Buddhist teaching, where sayings are used as instructions to direct the mind to respond differently. This practice is beautifully described by Pema Chodron.)

A wonderful instruction to work with in difficult relationships is: *Never give up on a person.* A beautiful counterpart of this is: *Never give up on yourself.*

How easy it is to give up on others (and on ourselves) when our expectations aren't met. The minute this happens, remind yourself of the instruction and take a deep breath. Return to the relationship with patience, compassion, and watchfulness.

We are helped in this practice by the virtue of doing zazen; by sitting still through all kinds of conditions, we learn to remain steadfast in the face of everything. We do not give up on anything, but are open, available, able to accompany the person with whatever they are going through rather than having to change or control him.

As we practice with this kind of "open-heartedness" it soon becomes obvious that the way we treat another is the way we also treat ourselves. That which we find ugly or unacceptable in another is simply a reflection of something we find ugly or unacceptable in ourselves.

Exercise 2: Naikan (Part II)

When working with relationships, the second part of Naikan (see chapter 6) is very good to focus on. Make a daily list of what you have given that day. Usually we think we are giving all day long, so it can be quite a surprise to be concrete and specific and see what we actually gave to whom. Perhaps less than we thought. Perhaps more.

This practice keeps us very conscious of what we are actually giving back to others. If it is not enough, we will feel prompted to give more, and be happy when the opportunities arise rather than resentful. If we are giving a great deal and become conscious of it, this itself brings contentment.

We can also do this practice on a specific relationship. What have I given to this person, day by day, year by year? We can start from when we first knew them, and at each sitting do three years at a time. This keeps us awake and aware.

Exercise 3: Making Friends with the Unacceptable

- Become aware of the qualities you find ugly or unacceptable in others. (Write them down if you wish.)
- Realize that these are qualities that also exist within yourself.
- Make peace with these qualities, both within and without.

The more we hide from, ignore, or repress aspects of ourselves and project them onto others, the more power these qualities have over us, and the greater likelihood they will appear in our lives as symptoms, bad dreams, or repetitive situations, which we feel we have no control over. Robert Bly calls this the *shadow aspect of human life*. He says that we dump all unacceptable parts of ourselves into our unconscious, hide from it, and let it fester there. Then we see these qualities in individuals and situations around us.

Exercise 4: Eat Your Shadow

In order to be free of this process, we must "eat our shadow." This means we must reclaim and own these hidden qualities, realize they are part of us, and welcome them into our lives. The very act of welcoming certain qualities or people takes the steam out of them. We can then absorb the energy and transform them into something constructive.

Zen practice is the practice of doing this—eating the shadow, sitting, and knowing that we ourselves contain the entire world.

CASE 21: (FROM *MUMONKAN*— TRANSLATED AS *THE GATELESS GATE*)

Koan: Ummon's Toilet Paper

THE CASE
A monk asked Ummon, "What is Buddha?"
    Ummon replied, "Toilet paper!"

MUMON'S COMMENT
"Ummon was too poor to prepare plain food, too busy to speak from notes. He hurriedly took up Toilet Paper to support the Way."

MUMON'S VERSE

Lightning flashing,
Sparks shooting;
A moment's blinking,
Missed forever.

Are you separating the holy and profane? Are you looking for a great, enlightened being to love, not a piece of toilet paper?

CHAPTER 9

AMBITION: TAMING THE VIOLENT MIND

ZEN MIRACLE 9
Our addiction to hatred fades away.

If you want to know if it's pure gold
You must see it through the fire.
                                    —*Ancient Zen saying*

The fire of ambition and anger burns deeply within. By ambition we mean the craving for power over others, the way a drug addict craves his drug. This craving makes us feel as if we feel we must conquer the world, conquer our enemies, lovers, and the parts of ourselves we reject. In other traditions, this fire is described as hell, where we burn when our lives have not been "good."

EXPRESSING ANGER

Psychologically speaking, in our culture, anger is often encouraged and valued. Clients are encouraged to express the anger they feel, "assert" themselves in opposition to others, stand up for their rights. When a person becomes able to do this, he or she is considered to be healthy, not a victim of abuse. Those who cannot stand up for their rights or assert themselves are thought to have weak ego structures and poor boundaries. Some are described as *masochists*—those who enjoy being punished, as a way to relieve unconscious guilt. In this frame of reference anger is seen as an expression of strength, a way to protect a fragile self.

ANGER IS A GREAT AFFLICTION

From the Zen point of view, anger is one of the three poisons, a great affliction. The rush we get from anger is counterfeit, a substitute for real strength. And the fragile self it is seen to protect doesn't even really exist. It is a figment of our imagination. Others and ourselves can only be harmed by negative outbursts.

Anger is often justified by saying that some individuals are "bad" and deserve the punishment inflicted upon them. In fact, punishment is thought to straighten them up, give them due, or in some way or other teach the bad guys a lesson.

Zen rejects the hypothesis that individuals are either good or bad. Human life is fluid. Zen points to the fact that one moment we can be saints, the next moment, devils. Good turns to bad and the other way around—our lives can be described as a process that contains all permutations. As we practice we learn not to hate hell, but to recognize it for what it is and recognize the danger and pain it contains.

When anger and hate arise within us, when domination, cruelty, and ambition arise, we maintain balance and simply experience them for what they are. We do not repress and deny the energy, but experience it fully and let it go. To stay steady and centered during the experience of anger, not to lash out, is a mark of the ripened person.

The Possibility of Heaven or Hell

Each interaction we have with another presents the possibility of heaven or hell. As we grow we become able to choose our destination, to recognize that anger and ambition are afflictions, not treasures, and that they can be transmuted into pure gold.

For quite some time now, Frank had been unable to concentrate at work. He became restless, preoccupied and nervous when he had to stay at his desk for too long. He would get up, stroll the corridors, take long coffee breaks, and spend too much time at lunch. When he was called on the fact that his work was incomplete, he would flush with resentment, and make a show of working harder, always leaving mistakes behind. When criticized by superiors, he would smile strangely and look at the floor, saying nothing.

Finally, one morning, Frank's suppressed feelings of resentment burst forth. When his boss approached him once again with a stern expression, Frank punched him squarely in the face, knocking him to the floor.

"He deserved it," Frank claimed over and over. "This guy has been riding me. He never had a good word for me, no matter what I do. The more I do, the more faults he finds. I'm the victim of worker abuse. If he doesn't get off my back, I'm gonna sue."

At the hearing, one of the justifications for Frank's behavior was that he was finally expressing his anger directly, not allowing himself to be a doormat anymore. Frank claimed that his response was healthy, though the manner it came out might have been too extreme.

Frank viewed himself as the victim of an ungiving and cruel world. He did not see his part or participation in it. He did not see the ways in which he passively called forth others' negative responses. He only sought justifications for his behavior. Some others at the office even suggested that punching the boss was a breakthrough for him, and that in the future he should just learn to express his anger more consistently. They did not see the difference between constructive communication, and the fueling of an energy that takes us straight to hell.

When we condone and express anger, the fact that we can hurt others is minimized, or overlooked. Either we block out the feelings of others, or feel they deserve what they get. This entire configuration is based upon the dualistic model of seeing others in opposition to ourselves. Completely encased in our own self-centered interest, we see ourselves as the wronged victim. We then blame the other for our pain and want him or her to suffer as we do. Whatever it is we want for another inevitably comes back at us. If we people our world with opponents and enemies, we will be torn down at every turn. Addicted to revenge, we are placing ourselves in the very center of hell.

After the hearing, the question was tossed around at Frank's workplace for quite a while about who the victim and the victimizer was. From a Zen point of view, this question is off target. The victim and victimizer are one—and the culprit is the violent mind.

> In the heat of battle, silence is best.
> —*Lojong instruction*

The Nature of Self-Centered Mind

By its very nature the self-centered mind is violent, driven by the fierce desire to want good for ourselves and not for another, to protect our group—national, religious, sociological—and condemn others, to block out reality and superimpose fantasies upon whatever comes to us. This is an onslaught upon life itself. The self-centered mind is full of personal demands and then violent reactions when these demands are not met. It is as though we are living with a wild, raging tiger inside.

Fuels for the Violent Mind

There are various fuels the violent mind requires. Without these fuels, it will burn out. However, not recognizing what we are up against, we inadvertently feed the fire continually, then wonder why we are burning inside.

1. Fantasies and Daydreams

Psychologists claim that fantasies, dreams, and daydreams are a substitute for gratification that we cannot obtain in ordinary life. They are healthy and have a purpose, teaching us about our deeper needs and longings and point a direction for our life to take. Many hours are spent in psychotherapy analyzing these dreams and wishes, and finding how to get them met.

Zen says that fantasies and daydreams fuel the violent mind. When they run wild, as they often do, it is as though we are living with a loaded gun, without any safety controls. In addition, most of the so-called needs and wishes manufactured by these fantasies have nothing to do with what is true for us, or what is healthy. Because they are unreal, manufactured needs can never be met, but instead, tease and torture us relentlessly. As we use our life energy to fulfill these mirages, we eventually become full of despair. This causes us to lapse into further fantasies to replace the true satisfaction we cannot find. This vicious cycle provides endless fuel and energy for the crafty, violent mind.

As we dissolve false needs and wishes, we can see what our true needs are, and how to meet them easily. It is the nature of life to provide for real needs. Of course, when this happens, the violent mind has no place to stand.

2. The Wheel of Karma

As we live fueled by anger, it is inevitable that we repeat the same mistakes continually. So many individuals leave relationships vowing never to go through that pattern again. After what seems like a respite, they make a fresh start with someone who appears to be completely different, only to have the same old problems reappear. The violent mind has drawn the same thing in another guise. It cannot allow success or fulfillment. It cannot allow anything to grow.

This pattern is called the *repetition compulsion*, the compulsion to repeat the same errors and painful situations in an effort to master them and make them turn out right this time. In Zen it is called the *Wheel of Karma*, where we play out the same painful scenarios, sometimes for lifetimes. How do we get off this wheel we are tied to?

First, we must realize that the violent mind, within us, is dedicated to failure and destruction. The sooner we face and realize this, the stronger we will be. It is difficult for many to face that the enemy in their lives is inside of them.

As we practice, we dissolve the energy that keeps the wheel going and return the energy to our true selves. Practice dismantles all within us that keeps this wheel churning.

I Am Going to Kill You

One evening, a friend came to Kara's house and decided to kill her. In the beginning he just came for a visit. The two of them had always been close and, at first, nothing seemed out of the ordinary. It was a lovely evening. She welcomed him in, and the two of them sat down to eat the meal she had prepared.

Then suddenly, there was a tiny misunderstanding. Kara's friend flushed deeply and rage grew inside as both his hands started to shake. Kara leaned forward to correct what she said, but by then he could not hear her. Instead, he started to yell, "I'm going to kill you."

Kara was stunned.

"Right now," he continued. "I want you dead."

Kara began to tremble. She loved this person and knew he loved her as well.

"Sit down," she pleaded.

He could not hear, but started banging on the table.

Her first thought was to run to the phone for help.

"Don't even think of calling the police," he shouted.

Kara stood completely still, feeling real danger. She couldn't understand how he could want to kill her when he loved her so much.

We do love one another and yet flames arise when the violent mind is not extinguished. Kara had been a Zen student for a while and had worked on a koan about what she would do if death came to her suddenly. Her teacher's question resonated now.

"What would you do if in one shocking moment your life was at stake? You had to act instantly. What would you do?"

Kara had sat with this. As she worked on it she thought, *This will never happen to me. It couldn't.* Now, in the middle of this storm, this koan popped into her mind.

Zen practice is about life and death, shocking moments, rage arising, the demand for an instant response. Focused deeply now upon her koan, Kara's fear suddenly evaporated. She became quiet, focused. Then she just looked at her friend and said, "Okay."

The moment she did that, he stopped. It was over. His face fell flat.

Kara had gone into a condition where both hope and fear had vanished. She was ready at that moment to meet her death.

The friend began crying, "I don't know what came over me."

Kara also started crying. They sat and cried together for a while. After they stopped crying, they went into the kitchen and had a bowl of soup.

WHAT IS REAL HERE?

What is real here? Is the rage real or the love underneath? Moments like this come to all of us, one way or another. Many times we are faced with people who we think are coming to harm us. We must call upon resources we may not know we have. How do we react? Do we call for the police? Do we escalate the violence? Do we give in to hatred?

These may be natural reactions, but at moments of danger, if we can become totally present, at one with ourselves and the other, another outcome may be possible. That state of being itself can harmonize and change many things. That state of being arises out of an accumulation of years of practice. Who knows what would have happened if Kara hadn't been able to be in that state at that moment? There could have been no turning back. One person in a clear condition can put an end to a potentially harmful chain of events.

Kara's ability came out of an accumulation of years of practice. That state of mind can happen to anyone at any moment, though, but when we practice, it becomes a more accessible part of ourselves.

So, when danger comes, how do you handle it? Danger doesn't have to be a moment of harm, it can be facing the loss of a love, of health, of money. There are many moments when what is important to us is suddenly taken away. A person in a clear condition of mind can dissolve many dangerous possibilities.

One of the aspects of this practice is learning how not to react but to respond. As we practice, we become very responsive, but we don't react with a knee-jerk reaction. The word *respond* comes from responsible, able to respond. Awake, available. We also practice immovability, so whatever comes up we can stay centered.

This is a lifelong practice that has many aspects to it. Let us look at what else is needed to harness the fierce energy of the violent mind:

> If you don't go into the tiger's cave
> How can you get a tiger cub?
> —*Ancient Zen saying*

Go Into the Tiger's Cave

Essentially, we must go into the tiger's cave. We must enter within ourselves and become aware of the raging forces that direct our lives and the lives of those we touch. We must be willing to be with our own violence, to see it, to smell it, to feel it, and to own it. We must have the ultimate courage not to project it outside ourselves and perceive a world of enemies who we grow to hate, judge, hurt, and reject. When we fall into the grip of this (as we all do, inevitably), we must become aware as soon as it is happening, and stop it on the spot. Usually, it is not the truth we are perceiving but the distortions of our own violent mind.

This takes time, but if we practice consistently, one day the power the violent mind uses to keep its hold over us becomes greatly diminished. There are even times when it disappears completely. At that very moment heaven appears. Then the violent mind turns into what it always was, absolutely nothing but a madman's dream. We then see we have given it all the power it had by our belief in it, and by our attention. By not looking at what was real.

ATTENTION! ATTENTION! ATTENTION!

A monk asked the Master, "What is the essence of Zen practice?"

The Master wrote a word on paper. It said, ATTENTION!

"Is that all?" the monk asked, incredulously.

Once again the Master wrote on the paper, ATTENTION! ATTENTION!

Still the monk hoped for more. "That's it? That's all?"

Filled with utter kindness, the Master wrote one last time: ATTENTION! ATTENTION! ATTENTION!

That's it!

HOLD YOUR SEAT

Another way of expressing this is done by a wonderful Lojong instruction:

Hold Your Seat.

This means to sit, stay centered, don't move, don't react. If something comes at you, allow it to come, and allow it to go. *Hold Your Seat* also means, if you fall down or make a mistake, come back again and get on the cushion. As you do that, over time you take back the power that you have attributed to the transitory world, which can push us and pull us like a leaf in the wind. This Lojong instruction means become imperturbable in the center of all storms. Become a container to include all. These teachings, or sayings, can be utilized in any situation in life—with your boss, your friend, your children. As you practice, you see that an angry person doesn't necessarily hate you or want to kill you. It's only phenomena, arising and falling that we make solid and important. We make it real by the story we tell ourselves and others about it, over and over again.

A related Lojong instruction is:

Be a child of illusion.

Lighten up. To think that everything will always be the same is illusion. Something new will always come and then it will go. If you can hold your seat, and see it as illusion, you won't get seasick, rocked around so much, throwing up over the edge of the boat. Instead you will be able to pay attention and enjoy the ride. Kara saved herself and her friend by being able to hold her seat.

The Tree Roshi

There was once a Zen Master who lived very simply in a tree. He did zazen in the branches, ate berries and nuts, and was content. Little by little his reputation grew and people sought him out for guidance. The Tree Roshi said nothing to anyone, just continued his simple life and practice of zazen. Finally, he consented to come out of the tree for a day and answer a question. The crowd had many questions, but they all boiled down to a simple one, "What is the essence of this practice. What is it all about?"

The Tree Roshi said, "Do only good. Do no harm to anyone."

The people were disappointed. "That's it? We all know that. Even a baby knows it."

"Even a baby knows it," said the Tree Roshi, "but even an eighty-year-old man cannot do it."

Words are easy, but to truly do no harm to any form of life, including oneself, is another matter. It is a lifelong practice. How do we actually undertake the great practice of the Tree Roshi?

DISSOLVING ANGER

Along with sitting through anger bravely and allowing it to run its course, we work with it carefully as it arises in everyday life.

A monk sat in zazen on a mountain for many years. He attained a state of *samadhi* (oneness), and felt deep peace and equanimity. After a time he went down from the mountain and back to the city, where the true test of his practice came. As soon as someone spoke to him rudely, anger and pride flared inside of him. How dare they treat someone like me that way? he exclaimed.

Does this mean that his time on the mountain was useless? No. It simply means that the roots of anger can go deep. Whatever melted on the mountain, melted. What he found inside him back on the streets, was still there to be extinguished. In and of itself anger is not bad. It is what we do with it that matters. If we let it run us, lash out and harm, that produces danger. If, however, we become senior to the anger, simply experience it for what it is, before long it will melt away. Fortunately for the monk, after many years of practice, he was in a position to laugh at himself and move along.

Anger can become our best friend if it forces us to be vigilant. If we did not have problems and afflictions, there would be no need to practice or understand the true essence of compassion and how to extend it to others.

One of the things we learn as we practice is to notice all aspects of our anger and how it works upon others and ourselves. This itself dissolves anger, just paying attention, just noticing.

3. Tricks the Violent Mind Plays

Another powerful fuel for the violent mind are the tricks it loves to play. These tricks keep us confused, not realizing what's behind them, or what's really going on.

SELF-SABOTAGE

The violent mind does not simply lash out at others, it enjoys self-sabotage as well. We start a piece of work and then stop in the middle, or spoil efforts we have made. We judge our efforts poorly and decide whatever we did was worthless and that it's better to stop. We decide we're too good for this person, or activity. For no reason at all, we become bloated with pride.

PRIDE

Our false sense of worth, pride, is another powerful fuel for the violent mind. This false ego arises because we have no basic idea of how great our beauty and value really are. Feeling worthless, we create a grandiose image of ourselves that must be constantly catered to and applauded. This image (or ego) demands endless attention and praise whether it deserves it or not. It demands to be loved, acknowledged, needed, and valued. This demand is made so intensely, because deep down it knows itself to be false, and that it can be overturned easily. Deep down it lives with the terror that others will find out that it is nothing but a figment of the imagination. This anguish of being nothing is the most intense anguish of all. It is the sense of not being real.

A way of withdrawing the fuel from this aspect of the violent mind is to know our true value, to make fabrications a thing of the past. How do we know our true value? Through what we have accomplished, our feelings, actions, through the loving eyes of another? This is knowing ourselves from the outside in. This is wanting corroboration, affirmation, acknowledgment from the outside world. Living that way our entire lives may thus be spent looking in the mirror of another's eyes. When we do not see what we like, anger burns strongly.

A wonderful antidote to this false pride are the words of the great Master Dogen Zenji:

> Life Is One Continuous Mistake.
> —*Dogen Zenji*

One Continuous Mistake

If we are truly able to absorb this statement it becomes much easier to become real. One continuous mistake relieves us of false feelings of shame, guilt, and self-hate when we fumble and err. It boldly and clearly informs us that the very nature of life itself forces us to fall down, make mistakes, be made a fool of, and then to get up again. It is this very process of life itself that diminishes foolish pride we are so filled with.

During my life and Zen practice if there has been a pothole in the street, like clockwork, I fall into it. If there was a mistake to be made, I made it. Not only once, but again and again. Instead of fearing to walk out of the house, I have learned to enjoy being in the potholes when I land there and spend time looking around. Rather than hating myself or the potholes, I just simply say, "Oh, blind again."

After fully experiencing a particular pothole, as many times as I fall in, getting out becomes easier. By now I have become quite good at falling into potholes and just climbing out. As a result of all this, I am quite familiar with the terrain of potholes and find a particular beauty in them. As I have done this many times, they hold less attraction to me. Now I fall in and get out in a matter of moments, no damage, no shame.

When we let go of guilt, shame, and the unnecessary pride involved in being right, not making mistakes, we are free to fall in or climb out, enjoy and learn from both activities. We are also free to give up our pride, relax deeply, and drink a cup of green tea.

ONE CUP OF GREEN TEA

Drinking a cup of
green tea,
I stopped the war.
                    —*Paul Reps*, Zen Telegrams

What is this green tea? How can we learn how to drink it? In order to really drink a cup of green tea, to stop the war, within and without, we must first become receptive. We must deeply appreciate the cup it is served in, and the efforts of those who bring it to us. Our mouths must be empty enough to taste this cup of tea. Of course we cannot just gulp it down. Sip by sip we receive it. We honor the green tea and it honors us. This is the only way the tea can stop the war that rages within us.

Once we become simple and aware the violent mind is exposed for the lie it is, and the harm it is doing. Then it is not so hard to just drop it. We drop the false notion that the outside world and the people in it are enemies to be conquered, demeaned, or harmed in anyway. We let go of wanting our good from another or feeling they can get in the way.

It is a shocking moment to realize that we are all truly one, subject to exactly the same longings and pressures, brothers and sisters, living briefly on this earth.

An excerpt from a beautiful poem by Thich Nat Hanh, the great Zen Master involved with engaged Buddhism, expresses this deeply.

Promise me,
promise me this day
while the sun is just overhead

Even as they strike you down
With a mountain of hate and violence
Remember, brother,
Man is not our enemy
And one day, when you face
This beast alone,
Your courage intact, your eyes kind
Out of your smile
Will bloom a flower

ZEN IN ACTION

Exercise 1: Face Each Other and Smile

Here is a wonderful exercise created by Thich Nat Hanh, included in *Being Peace*. When disharmony exists in the Sangha, or among the body of monks, this is what he does to dispel it. Naturally this exercise can be applied to any group of individuals.

A. All sit facing each other quietly and smile. This smile represents their willingness to be friendly to one another. Before anything at all can be done, there must be mutual willingness to help, not fight. Basic intention is primary.

B. The individuals in conflict know everyone expects them to make peace. No one listens to stories spread by others, or spreads news of the conflicting monks.

C. *Remembrance*—Each monk remembers the entire history of the conflict, every detail. All sit patiently and listen to each as they take their turn. In this way *all* thoughts and feelings are included, from both sides of the conflict.

D. *Nonstubbornness*—All expect peace and do their best to create an atmosphere for it. Atmosphere of the assembly is crucial.

E. *Covering mud with straw*—A senior monk is appointed to each side of the conflict. Each says something to the assembly to deescalate the conflict. Whatever they say is respected. They speak to cause the others to understand their monk more fully. In this case hard feelings are dissipated. Mud is the conflict, straw is lovingkindness.

F. *Voluntary confession*—Each monk reveals his own short-comings and apologizes.

G. *Sacrifice*—All are reminded that the welfare of the entire community is most important. Each monk must make a sacrifice and be ready to accept the verdict.

H. *Accepting verdict*—The decision is made and each monk must do various things to repair what has happened. Community must accept it. Harmony is thus restored.

This beautiful process is a fine description of Zen practice in action. It includes great respect for all parties concerned, no blame, hatred or harsh judgment, but a fair and deep hearing of all aspects of the situation. The emphasis is not upon who is right and who is wrong. Instead the emphasis is upon how harmony will be restored. The expectation and desire of all is for harmony, not retribution. Each party to the conflict takes responsibility for their own part in it, publicly acknowledging their shortcomings and apologizing. In this manner no one is put to shame, both take part together, and forgiveness and compassion are the order of the day. The conflict becomes a great teaching where one has the opportunity to learn, grow, share with others, and dissolve false righteousness and pride.

CHANGING ONE HEART AT A TIME

Needless to say, if we all lived in this manner, there would never be a need for senseless killing or war. Our inner and outer resources could naturally go to making this world a place where all could thrive mutually. Zen works with one person at a time. As one heart changes, it affects the next. Old, fixed, frozen attitudes we carry toward one another, fueled by delusion and fear, melt naturally. Zen understands that every person who appears before you is just another part of yourself. You have attracted this person only to see yourself a little better. And, most important, what you reject in another, you must also be hiding from and rejecting in yourself.

Exercise 2: The Turnaround Procedure

Another simple and beautiful exercise helps individuals and couples in conflict reach mutual understanding quickly and easily. The individuals in conflict should write out a little scene that depicts the essence of the problem they're having. Now each should take the role of their opponent and act the scene out for others to see. They must not play their own part, but see and play the situation out through the eyes of their adversary. Before very long their understanding will increase. Their fixed point of view and position is broken through. They cannot help but understand fully what the other is going through. New solutions arise in this process quickly. It is fun to do and will be surprising to you.

Exercise 3: Naikan (Part III)

In working with anger, the third question of the Naikan exercise is powerful. Everyday we ask ourselves, "What trouble or pain have I caused to another?" Or, in reflecting on a relationship, we focus on this part.

Usually we focus upon the wrongs others have done us, how we have been misused or maligned. When we control the focus of the mind, and become aware of how we may have inadvertently hurt another, or caused them trouble we were not conscious of, our own anger and righteousness dissolves. Instead we become eager to correct our errors and amend our ways. The purpose of this exercise is not to create guilt, but to redirect our focus away from our usual point of view.

Everything is part of the creation and contains all aspects. Within each creation the Buddha Nature exists—the ability to grow, be enlightened. Why should anything be rejected? The more we separate and confine the world by our dualistic thinking, the more we label, divide, and categorize, the more constricted our experience of life becomes. We become prisoners in jails of our own making, and take others as prisoners as well. Zazen is the key to opening our jail cell, to allowing dualistic thinking to subside.

Here is a famous koan that deals with the mind that cuts and separates.

CASE 14: (*GATELESS GATE*)
Koan: Nansen Cuts the Cat in Two

Nansen Osho saw monks quarreling over a cat. He held up the cat and said, "If you can give an answer, you will save the cat. If not, I will kill it." No one could answer, and Nansen cut the cat in two.

That evening Joshu returned, and Nansen told him of the incident. Joshu took off his sandal, placed it on his head, and walked out.

"If you had been there, you would have saved the cat," Nansen remarked.

MUMON'S COMMENT
"Tell me, what did Joshu mean when he put the sandal on his head? If you can give a turning word on this, you will see that Nansen's decree was carried out with good reason. If not, "Danger!"

MUMON'S VERSE
> Had Joshu been there,
> He would have done the opposite;
> When the sword is snatched away,
> Even Nansen begs for his life.

What is it that we cut in two by our quarreling and dualistic thinking? How can this be overturned? This koan comes to show us the very nature of the tangled mind.

PART THREE

LETTING GO

CHAPTER 10

GRASPING AND HOLDING ON

ZEN MIRACLE 10
We can empty our cup.

A student sought out a great Zen Master to discover the secrets of this universe and what his life truly meant. He traveled far and wide and finally located a Master living simply in a hut on top of a mountain. The student made his way to the hut and the Master welcomed him in. The hut was furnished sparsely and was immaculate. The Master motioned for him to sit down on a mat on the floor and went to boil water for tea. The student had to wait for the tea to be ready.

The water boiled slowly. The student grew restless, eager to get the preliminaries over with, ask his question, and get his answer to the true meaning of the universe. He wasn't hungry for tea, he was hungry for an answer. He thought he could get it just like that. He thought the answer was something someone could give him.

The more restless he grew, the more slowly the water boiled. Not only was it clear that the student had not acquired patience, it was also clear, as he waited, that he was not at home with himself. He thought some answer presented by the teacher was going to put him at rest.

117

Finally the tea was ready. The Master gave the student a teacup and the student trembled excitedly. His mind and body were not stable. In fact he began to have more and more thoughts of additional questions he could ask after the Master answered this one.

The Master began to pour the tea, up to the very top of the cup. Even though the cup was filled to the brim, the Master kept on pouring, so that very soon the hot tea spilled over the edges and onto the student's trembling hands.

"What are you doing?" the student cried out.

"What are you doing?" the Master replied. "Just like this teacup you are full of yourself, full of opinions, desires, questions, imagination. How can you receive anything from me when your cup is so full? In order to receive any teaching, first you must empty your cup."

In order to receive the truth of Zen, we must be willing to empty our cup, let go of our vain imaginings, become able to taste and appreciate a simple cup of tea. We do not sit before the Master trembling, thinking he has some kind of answer that will make our lives all right. Little by little we begin to realize that this cup of tea contains everything.

Holding on to Everything

We come into life empty-handed and then expect to grab and hold on to everything. Immediately we make claims for ownership: "This is my mother. She can't go away." Some enormous hunger begins to develop. What exactly are we hungering for? First, it is only food and love that we are demanding. In the beginning it may be easy to find satisfaction, but soon this craving grows more subtle. Our so-called needs become more intricate.

We want everything. We want to receive, to hold and possess. We want to have everything and to have it forever. A little child in the store does not know what to grab at first. He takes whatever he sees. He feels his toys belong only to him. His friends are his possessions as well. The child insists they may not go away. This kind of attitude is hard to outgrow.

When change comes we see it as a villain taking our goodies away. But what do we own? In truth, what really belongs to us? Even our bodies have a life of their own. Sooner or later we will have to return them to the universe.

There are many kinds of foods we require as we grow into maturity—emotional, intellectual, social, and spiritual food. The journey of our lives may be said to be the act of discovering the different kinds of foods we need for nourishment, how to get it, digest, and absorb it. And then we have to let go, give back. We could not live very long if we did not go to the bathroom.

Few like to talk about the bathroom, but it is very important if we are going to talk about attachment and letting go. No one can live just eating and consuming forever. We must learn to be satisfied and let go. We must learn how to digest what we take in, find that which is nourishing, and discard the waste. This is the very process of life.

We must stop and look at what are we willing to return to the universe. Certainly not those we love, certainly not our own precious lives. We do not realize that much of the pain of life comes from taking and not being willing to give back.

Many lives are centered around accumulation, taking, and holding on. But soon we are full and overflowing. We are so full we can hardly move. It is not so easy to stop and let go, to clean out our homes and lives.

After several rocky love affairs, Lester came to therapy and said, "I only want a stable relationship. Help me get one."

The therapist said, "If I had them to give out I'd give one to everyone."

WANTING TO BE SECURE

Psychologically speaking, we want situations that are comfortable and secure. We want to know what to expect from the other and not have to suffer the pain of alternation and change.

But what is truly stable? In the world of phenomena there is nothing but change, and still we demand stability from it. When a therapist agrees that a client must find or create a "stable" relationship, the therapist becomes part of the illness, because it is madness to long for something that is contrary to the nature of life itself. The real question is what makes us truly stable, able to withstand the inevitable winds of loss and change.

In Zen we say,

Dwelling as change itself, brings peace.

—Ancient Zen saying

This simply means not expecting to control life, but knowing that every moment will be new. Psychologically speaking, we compartmentalize. Part of us knows there is nothing but change, and yet we still want everything to stay the same. If we sit long enough we realize that our bodies change, our thoughts change, winter passes into spring. By dwelling as change itself we receive the ability to accept and deal with change and loss of all kinds.

Most struggle against the fact of impermanence. When this becomes extreme it leads to constriction, obsession, addiction, anything to hold on. For most people the experience of change is psychologically equivalent to the experience of loss. There's a normal grieving period that usually goes on when something precious is taken away. During this period of grieving, many do not allow themselves to realize that something new is always on the way.

CHANGE MUST COME

From the Zen point of view change is release, it is inevitable. We are change. Change is not failure. When something changes in a person's life that they haven't initiated they may feel like they've failed, that there's something wrong with them. As people get older they can become encrusted, calling the change they've experienced disappointment. Their lives become smaller and narrower. They meet fewer people, walk fewer blocks, take the same vacations with the same friends every year. They do not want to experience any more change. The life force in this person becomes diminished. Living an encrusted life causes both physical and mental illness. In these cases it's the psychological self causing difficulties, by demanding life to go its way and refusing to look more deeply at the nature of life as it is. Healing is opening up to the power and also to the beauty of change, letting go of our fear of it.

What Do We Own?

After Randy's best friend stole his fiancée away, he discovered they had been having a secret affair for several months. Despondent and in deep shock Randy came for therapy. He arrived in a state of suspiciousness and sat in the office in despair, convinced he could never trust again. In fact, what had happened became proof to him that the whole world was against him, others were secretly out to get him, laughing at him, and enjoying his misery. He said he could tell by the look in their eyes.

While this may seem like an extreme reaction, the development of paranoia is not as uncommon as one may think. In fact, it could be considered a way of life for many in our society. Many feel that it is wise to distrust others, question their motives, refuse to trust once they have been burned and live life fearing the worst. Catastrophic expectations are common. People who engage in them are seen as smart and crafty, likely to get ahead. They do not ask ahead of what, or what toll this takes upon them.

Many psychological illnesses arise from the experience of loss—loss of love, job, people, money, youth, position, reputation. This need to protect our belongings and our pride runs most people's lives. Distrust of others arises, fearing they want to take our good away. Stinginess of heart develops, constricting all aspects of lives. Some live in the torment of constant suspiciousness imputing bad motives to all. From the psychological point of view, this is a projection of an individual's own hatred, the result of living in bad faith.

Paranoia is the epitome of dualistic thinking—the extreme split into a world of black and white, good and bad, subject and object. The other is seen as the enemy. *I have to fight them to get what I need, protect my turf and must be vigilant against disasters that are lurking everywhere.* Individuals caught in the grip of this mental condition live in a world peopled by opponents, always on their guard. Their lives become a defense against being hurt, robbed, or made a fool of. They have no awareness of their own negativity or how they project it into the world and do not realize that it is their state of mind that creates their hell. For these individuals, *forgiveness* (a form of letting go) is often impossible. Their entire lives are based on holding on to the wrongs done to them, getting revenge, hiding, and secrecy. This decision to hold on to negative experience, dwell, and expand upon it, is the basis of the paranoid mind.

RETURNING TO THE ROOT

When we return to the root, we gain the meaning.
When we pursue external objects, we lose the reason.
Transformations going on in an empty world which
    Confronts us
Appear real all because of ignorance
                            —*Sosan*, On Believing in Mind

We know we are all leaves on a tree, but do not know the root that sustains us. One leaf turns to another for comfort, not realizing that the other leaf is also blowing in the wind. As one leaf tries to gain nourishment from another, it loses its stability. When each leaf on the tree returns to the root, it will feel secure no matter which way the wind is blowing, or how the other leaves are blowing as well. Once the single leaf realizes it is part of the tree, it becomes aware of its natural pattern—a time to bud, blossom, change color, and then finally blow away in the wind. No problem. The process is not in the leaf's control. A leaf is simply a leaf, though deeply connected to the profound roots of the tree it grows on. Now it can enjoy its life as a leaf, no matter what stage it is in. It can also enjoy the other leaves and the golden wind that blows through all the branches causing them all to blow away when autumn is done.

All Composite Things Must Decompose

All composite things must decompose, disappear.
—*the Buddha*, The Diamond Sutra

This is a primary teaching of the Buddha. That which comes together, sooner or later, must part. No need to call it abandonment, it is simply the nature of the world of appearances. The problem isn't with life itself, but with our desire to base our security and sense of self-worth upon that which is fleeting and refusal to see that dewdrops are dewdrops and cannot be clung to. If we persist in a life like this, can we have anything else but disappointment and pain?

If we persist in spending our whole life trying to hold everything together we will develop a sense of hopelessness. No matter how much we try, everything constantly falls apart. It has to. That is its very nature. It is the meaning of impermanence itself.

Our false sense of security is at best only a holding action. It is based upon that which is not real. The fragile rowboat we swim through life in is constantly tipping. It cannot hold up. Sooner or later, we must realize it is made only of cardboard. Is there a real ship we can board somewhere? Can we let go of the oars and become one with the ocean?

Most of us cannot. We feel the tighter we hold on the less frightened we will be. The opposite is true. The gripping itself creates the fear. The more Randy clings, frets, and hides in self-created isolation, the more fearful the outside world begins to seem. This behavior itself causes the terror.

Nothing to Hold On To

The tighter we hold on, the more we crush whatever it is in the palm of our hand. This crushing and being crushed is at the core of the pain we experience in life. It is our resistance to the flow of life, and our terror of being abandoned. As we practice diligently, a miraculous awareness dawns. For some it dawns suddenly, for others it is gradual. But dawn it must, as we keep sitting. We realize we can never be abandoned, that we are loved, cared for, and protected. It was just by clinging to the outside world that we abandoned ourselves. When we do not grasp or cling we become available to the endless resources the universe constantly supplies. It is simply a matter of opening our hearts and hands, and seeing for ourselves.

Understanding Attachment

Why are these simple truths so hard to practice? Why do we attach and cling so tenaciously? Attachment seems so automatic, natural, and fundamental that we do not question it at all. Attachment is usual, but not natural. Certainly, it is not necessary. It arises out of our deep confusion about who we are, the nature of our lives itself, and where we are ultimately going. It arises out of a misunderstanding about the nature of relationships and a false fear of being abandoned.

Attachment and holding on provide a false sense of security, giving us the illusion that the world is stable and real. Somehow we cannot really fathom the powerful words of the Diamond Sutra, which tell us otherwise:

Thus shall ye think of all this fleeting world:
A star at dawn, a bubble in a stream;
A flash of lightning in a summer cloud,
A flickering lamp, a phantom, and a dream.
                              —*the Buddha*, The Diamond Sutra

No one wants to be a dewdrop, a bubble, or a flash of lightening. We want to be the center of the universe. And, in fact, we are, though not in the way we imagine. No matter what we wish to hold on to, the bubble we are keeps on bursting and changing. Our hair grows thinner, our children leave us, our mates grow weary and look elsewhere for love. That which was once exciting, fades. We try to pretend this isn't happening and desperately struggle to keep everything the same. It is as if we were in the wild ocean in a tiny rowboat bobbing up and down.

Dancing As Long As I Can

A beautiful woman in her early sixties, Thalia, went dancing on Saturday nights in the summer in Central Park. She put on her long, flowing dress, brushed her colored hair, and stood at the sidelines, waiting for a partner.

"This lull will only last for a little while," she said to a friend who had accompanied her. "Even though it's harder these days, most of the time someone asks me to dance. I'm proud of that."

This particular night the lull continued for quite a while. Thalia smiled wanly and said, "When I was young and entered the dance hall, men turned to look at me. They crowded around me, I had my pick. When I was middle-aged, I turned to look at men, they smiled at me and came over. It wasn't so crowded, but there was never a lull. Now that I'm older, I look at them and they turn away. Still, two or three usually come by. You'll still see me out there tonight dancing. I'll keep dancing as long as I can, even though my legs are about to collapse."

Thalia must keep dancing to feel valuable, alive. Without the admiration of men, her life seems over. She'd rather collapse on the dance floor than sit alone in a room and face herself quietly.

Meeting the Dharma

It is lack of knowing who we truly are, the nature of the universe and our real place in it that causes us to hold on so tight. This is also called the study of *dharma*. Dharma is the essential truth about the nature of the universe and our lives in it. Once we grasp and digest this we never again feel alone. All the koans presented to students are one form or another of penetrating these truths—understanding who we are, what the world is, and what we are doing here.

As we practice we answer these koans by peeling off layer upon layer of social conditioning, encrusted beliefs, fears, and superstitions. Everyday life, too, presents its own precious koans, people we have difficulty with, situations and individuals we cannot let go or feel we have to control, repetitive patterns that keep us stuck in our lives, endless memories, yearnings, and dreams. The very process of Thalia's aging, and men looking away from her, is a tremendous koan life is giving her. How does she grapple with it? By denying the facts of her life? By continuing to smile and dance though her legs are collapsing? Others deal with this koan by getting facelifts, dating younger people, leaving their spouse after many years. How else can this koan be lived through? How can we come to the center of it, so that it permits us to live with equanimity, not to see life as a robber, coming to take our youthful beauty away. Here is the way the nun Chiyono handled the koan Thalia is confronting.

No More Water in the Pail

When the nun Chiyono studied Zen under Bukko of Engaku she was unable to attain the fruits of meditation for a long time. At last one moonlit night she was carrying water in an old pail bound with bamboo. The bamboo broke and the bottom fell out of the pail, and at that moment Chiyono was set free. In commemoration she wrote a poem:

> In this way and that I tried to save the old pail
> Since the bamboo strip was weakening and about to break
> Until at last the bottom fell out,
> No more water in the pail!
> No more moon in the water!
>
> —*Zen Flesh, Zen Bones*

The pail, the water, and Chiyono gone. What is Thalia hoping for?

ZEN IN ACTION

Exercise 1: What We Cling To

This is an exercise in becoming aware of what we cling to, and what we truly need now. Make a list of those things in your life you are greatly attached to. Stop and look it over, see what purpose they serve for you. What would happen if you let go of one of them?

Each day this week, let go of one, just for the day. See how it feels. You may be surprised.

Exercise 2: What Is Truly Valuable

What is truly valuable to you? Make a list of those things that are particularly valuable to you at present. What purpose are they serving? What was valuable to you five years ago? Ten years ago? Tomorrow? Notice the changes. Allow them to be.

Exercise 3: Finding Your True Way

Take a moment and see how you view your life and death. What do you believe, fear, or expect about them? Where are you headed, where is your true home? Do these thoughts serve you? Are they stopping other aspects of your life? Do they bring compassion and strength?

Stop another moment and ask yourself what you *really* know about your life and death? What is the danger, *really?* Why do you live as if there were one?

CASE 3: (FROM *HEKIGANROKU*— TRANSLATED AS *THE BLUE CLIFF RECORDS*)

Koan: Baso's Sun-Faced Buddha, Moon-Faced Buddha

The great Master Baso was seriously ill. The chief priest of the temple came to pay his respects. He asked, "How do you feel these days?"

The Master said, "Sun-faced Buddha, Moon-faced Buddha."

SETCHO'S VERSE

Sun-faced Buddha! Moon-faced Buddha!
For twenty years I have had fierce struggles,
Descending into the dragons' cave for you.
The hardship defies description.
You clear-eyed monks—don't make light of it.

Among the many Buddhas are the Sun-faced Buddha, said to live for eighteen hundred years, and the Moon-faced Buddha, said to live for a day and a night. This saying of Baso's, "Sun-faced Buddha, Moon-faced Buddha," stands out conspicuously among notable Zen sayings. Imagine you are watching the glorious setting sun at the far end of the ocean. Moment by moment, the golden-faced Buddha sinks below the horizon. No words can describe the glory and radiance of his face. Everything is condensed into this present moment. It is eternal. And again, imagine that, at midnight, you are watching the moon's mirrorlike face, inclined a little in her musing, poised over the mountains. Everything is silent. Her life may be only one day and one night, but this moment after moment's being truly represents real existence.

—*Katsuki Sekida*

What is Thalia? A sun-faced Buddha? A moon-faced Buddha? Why can't she realize?

CHAPTER 11

EMPTY HANDS

ZEN MIRACLE 11
We can empty our hands.

The great Zen Master Dogen Zejni went from Japan to China to study Zen. He spent years in a monastery studying and working with the monks. When he returned to his homeland he was asked what he brought back with him after so many years of study.

Dogen replied, "I have come back with nothing but empty hands."

Empty hands are powerful. They are the essence of Zen practice. When our hands are filled, closed, or grasping, they are useless. They cannot reach out to others, touch, comfort, lift, or bless. Closed hands are encumbered by all they cannot let go of. As we grow older possessions accumulate and our hands stiffen around to hold them tight. Memories besiege us, shakiness takes over, and many use their hands to simply hold on. They do not realize the strength and power of living with empty hands.

ONLY WANTING TO GIVE

When we only wanted to give, bear no grudges, and are not grasping at what we have, our hands become wide open, useful and flexible, holding on to nothing.

131

Develop a mind that dwells upon nothing.
> —*the Buddha*, The Diamond Sutra

Not only do our hands hold on to nothing, our mind can also let go. Along with zazen, there are other practices that help us develop this nondwelling mind, a mind that is supple and can give whatever has to be given and also take whatever comes. An important practice in developing this is called *dana paramita*—the practice of giving. But first we must understand what true giving and receiving are.

> Apples given,
> And oranges received in return.
> —*Shiki*

GIVING AND RECEIVING

The very act of giving and receiving freely opens up our hands and helps us let go. But few give freely. There can be many intentions when giving—to hold on to someone, to flatter, cajole, make someone dependent, to assert one's own power and control. This is not giving, but taking. Some give gifts that are too costly for them. Others cannot let anything go. Ultimately it is holding on that keeps all true nourishment away. A balance between true giving and receiving is vital. When one finds they cannot give or receive freely, it is time to look at what they are holding on to.

FIND WHAT IS VALUABLE

Why don't we stop and ask, "Is this valuable? Is this meaningful? Do I need or want this anymore?" Ryoken's life teaches us that the more you give, the more you will be able to receive the incredible moon that is constantly shining on us all.

True giving and receiving are one. When we give fully, without wanting anything in return, we become full. There is no giver or receiver there, only an open heart. Once we are able to offer to others, we will see that the world is continually offering itself to us as well.

We breathe in and breathe out every day. We take in air and return air to the universe. We have a dream and it fades. We wake up in the morning and sleep when night comes. Every step we take contains both giving and receiving, life and death. Something new arises, changes and passes away. In many moments of our lives we experience letting go, giving up naturally.

Zen practice asks us to realize that giving is not different from receiving, they are interlinked. If we give fully and completely, when the next moment comes we have room to receive what is next. Without breathing out, we cannot breathe in. In a sense this is the pulse of life and death itself. If we do not live out of interpretations, fantasies or explanations, there is nothing to fear about letting go.

> Someone said, "Life and death is here. How am I to cope with it?"
> Master Ummen said, "Where is it?"
>
> —*Ancient Zen saying*

We don't know what life and death are, what will happen if we give completely, what happens when we let go, where it will take us. In a similar manner, we have no real idea where we are headed ultimately, when time comes to let go of life itself. We cling to what is familiar as a way to feel grounded and secure, but this kind of security is based upon an illusion. The lives we are living in can fall apart easily. Everything can suddenly be taken away. How do we respond then? By holding on more tightly? By accumulating more and more?

The following beautiful saying by Ryoken advises,

> Return to your home,
> Purify your heart
> Ask nothing for yourself.

First we must know where this home is that we have to return to. How do we purify our hearts? What does it mean to "ask nothing for ourselves"? At first the answers may seem obvious, but if we live with these questions fully, we will realize a deeper direction in our lives.

Return to Your Home

Dana, a Zen student, had to go to California for about ten days. She said to her brother who was living there, "I'm packing lightly."

He said, "Yes, you're a Zen student, you should. But remember, it gets hot during the day, it gets cold at night. Bring sweaters for the evening, cool shirts for the afternoon. I'm warning you, the weather changes."

Suddenly she began thinking that if it gets that hot she'd probably need a bathing suit and summer dresses for the afternoon. For the evenings she'd need something different. And how about mornings before the sun rose? Her suitcase started filling up. She'd had a longing to go with a very small suitcase, but before long chose a larger one.

Her brother then called and asked her not to forget to bring along some old books he'd been wanting, and a package for mother. Soon Dana's luggage was bulging at the seams. As she packed she kept thinking of how in the zendo you needed so little and what a relief that was. In the early days at the zendo, another student had said that all he wanted to learn from this practice was to travel lightly. That had struck her. She thought about it now as her suitcase grew thicker. How long would it take to learn to travel lightly? She hadn't thought she needed so many things, but one thing she was certain she did need was the right room to stay in. It had to be quiet at night, and sunny in the daytime. That wasn't too much to ask.

> Of course we think we have the right to ask for many things, that it is important for certain needs to be met. In this frame of mind we do not understand the power of, *"Ask nothing for yourself."*

Dana then called her brother to confirm the hotel room he'd found for her.

"Even though I'm flexible," she reminded him, "please remember that I really need a room that's quiet to sleep in."

He said, "Of course. I'll make sure I get you a quiet room. Mom and I are looking forward to seeing you. Make sure you're here on time."

"Of course I'll be on time," she answered. "One more thing about the room, it can be small, I don't care, but if possible, I'd love the sun coming in, in the morning. I haven't been on a vacation for four or five years. That's not too much to ask, is it?"

The brother said, "No problem."

She said, "It's really important for me to have a quiet place to return to after a long day of running around."

Dana thought her peace would be back in the room, after a hectic day with her mother and brother.

Arrangements were carefully made. The plane taking the passengers to California was an hour late arriving. The doors didn't open when they arrived. Passengers had to wait an hour. Then there was something wrong with the fuel tank. They had to wait a few more hours and were then rerouted to another flight. By the time Dana got to the gate all the seats were taken. She was then switched to a different airline.

Fifteen hours later she arrived in Los Angeles and had to wait two more hours at the airport while her bags arrived on another plane. By the time she and her brother got to the hotel the room he'd chosen so carefully and reserved for her had been given to someone else.

"We didn't think you were coming," the man at the desk said.

To be a monk is to be a homeless one, one who is able to go wherever the wind blows, to be at home in whatever circumstances life provides. Dana was being tested and taught the true meaning of "*Return to your home.*"

She and her brother then began driving around late at night looking for a room. Every hotel was full. Finally, at the far end of town one room was available. Dana just barely got to sleep when she was awakened an hour later by a megaphone in a nearby stadium calling out names. She jumped out of bed. A graduation ceremony was going on in the stadium just under her room. People in the stands were cheering for each person called. She stood at the window staring.

When her brother arrived a few hours later she said, "We're checking out immediately."

The next night she was awakened by an earthquake. The room was rocking and people were screaming in the halls. She awoke, frantic, until she realized that life was giving her its own kind of sesshin. As the days passed she found herself in a different room every night.

One night she returned to her hotel one hour after checkout to find all of her clothing rolled into a plastic bag and thrown into the back of the lobby. The manager had checked her out.

She was getting the point slowly.

Her frantic brother kept asking, "Why is all this happening?"

"In Zen we don't ask that," Dana said. "We just take whatever comes."

"But there's got to be a reason all this is going on."

Most of us spend 95 percent of our lives trying to find out why. But ultimately, it's not the *why* that counts, but *how* one is going to be with all that happens. When one stays fully in the middle of experience, the answers come all by themselves.

What was happening to Dana was the epitome of Zen practice. The real koan she was receiving was could she include all of what is happening in the vacation and have a wonderful time.

As the trip drew to a close her brother said, "Thank God I'm not like you, needing a quiet room. I can sleep anywhere. Nothing bothers me. I'm just glad to lay down my head. But tonight, you'll sleep fabulously. I found a really quiet room in the back so you'll leave for the airport in the morning rested."

Dana said, "Great." She was relieved to be going home.

First thing in the morning, her brother called frantic, yelling into the phone, "You can't go to the airport. There's a bomber in town. There have been warnings. The airport is closed. I'll have to drive you to San Diego to catch a flight. I got a seat on a plane for you first thing tomorrow morning. You'll sleep in a hotel near the airport in San Diego tonight."

By now Dana was beginning to get it. "It doesn't matter," she said. "I don't need a quiet room. I'll sleep anywhere. Pick me up whenever you can."

Dana was preparing to return to her home.

Return to your home. Return to yourself. When we hear the bell in zazen it calls us home, asking us to take our attention back, to return from wandering in plans, fantasies, demands, expectations.

Purify your heart, ask nothing for yourself. That's a little harder. Most of our lives consists of asking for a lot. Real joy and contentment comes, however, when we are not filled with craving. Instead of asking to be filled, we ask to be used. This goes against the grain but we can try it little by little, just for an hour one day.

Purify your heart just by being still, by looking and letting yourself know who you are purification happens and we understand the Zen saying,

Place after place is the right place.

—*Ancient Zen saying*

Where is the road to Hanshan?
There is no road to Hanshan.

—*Ancient Zen saying*

Dana and her brother didn't start driving to San Diego until it was getting dark out. Her brother had booked a room in a tall hotel. They drove quietly, saying little. When they arrived in San Diego, they looked up and saw a wall of rooms looking down at them, with lights on in each of them. The two of them burst out into laughter. They sat in the car laughing and laughing, then finally got out and went into the hotel.

The Great Joke

What is the great joke they were laughing at? What is the mis-understanding Dana had lived with forever? Perhaps she suddenly realized that all of her searching had been in vain. Nothing was hidden, not now or ever. Before she had been unable to see it. Her endless demands had covered her eyes. Now, perhaps, she could dwell anywhere.

A mind that dwells upon nothing is another way of describing empty hands. It is a mind that is new and fresh each moment, able to be present for whatever appears. It does not stick to plans or dreams. It is not filled with hatred, memories, desires, and indignation about how others behave. Through tireless zazen, sitting by sitting, this mind develops all by itself.

Zen in Action

Exercise 1: Open Your Hands

See what your hands are filled with as you go through the days. What do you occupy them with? How heavy is it for you? Now simply practice opening up your hands. Put down what you're carrying in them. Let them be available.

Exercise 2: Ask Nothing for Yourself

Notice all that you ask for in every situation. How much of this is truly needed? Now, in one situation each day, practice asking nothing for yourself. See what you are receiving when you demand nothing at all. See what you are giving. See what the universe naturally provides.

Exercise 3: Dwell Upon Nothing

Become aware of where you are dwelling and what you are dwelling upon. Change your direction and dwell somewhere else. Now do it again and again. Whenever you feel stuck, frustrated, or limited, pick up and change your dwelling, and change what your mind is dwelling upon. Then take one step further and dwell upon nothing at all.

CASE 7: (FROM *MUMONKAN*— TRANSLATED AS *THE GATELESS GATE*)

Koan: Joshu's Wash Your Bowl

A monk said to Joshu, "I have just entered this monastery. Please teach me."

"Have you eaten your rice porridge?" asked Joshu.

"Yes, I have," replied the monk.

"Then you had better wash your bowl," said Joshu.

With this the monk gained insight.

MUMON'S COMMENT

"When he opens his mouth, Joshu shows his gallbladder. He displays his heart and liver. I wonder if this monk really did hear the truth. I hope he did not mistake the bell for a jar."

MUMON'S VERSE

Endeavoring to interpret clearly,
You retard your attainment.
Don't you know that flame is fire?
Your rice has long been cooked.

Once the rice is eaten, the bowl is washed. No need to linger, no need to dwell.

CHAPTER 12

PILGRIMAGE

ZEN MIRACLE 12
You can come and go freely.

> Coming from nowhere,
> I ring the bell
> Going to nowhere,
> I ring the bell.
> —*Master Fukei*

In many of the great religions there is an injunction to undertake a pilgrimage, to leave one's usual place, friends, activities, state of being, and journey forth to the unknown. This is the ultimate form of letting go, a journey to find God, the Self, the Infinite. It is a journey taken to break attachments, destroy habits, open our eyes, and find out what life really is and what our place is in it.

THE ESSENCE OF PILGRIMAGE

On another level, life itself can be viewed as a pilgrimage. We arrive, not knowing where we came from, and heading to an unknown destination. We do not know when we will arrive, what will await us, or what the effects of our time on this earth will be.

All is shrouded in mystery. This is a mystery we usually turn away from, believing our time here to be lengthy and stable, believing this world to be an end in itself.

The essence of a pilgrimage is to stop clinging to false habits, security, stability, and to be willing to surrender to the vast unknown. Even one sitting of zazen is a pilgrimage. We leave our possessions outside the zendo, sit down in one state of mind and do not know what will happen. We willingly enter the unknown recesses of our mind and heart.

> Coming, going, the waterfowl
> Leaves not a trace,
> Nor does it need a guide.
> —*Dogen Zenji*

Much personal discord and suffering comes because we are unwilling to view our lives and relationships as pilgrimages and journeys, designed to take us deeper into the mystery of who we are. Instead we demand control and consistency. We demand that life be reasonable. When our lives break apart, when we undergo losses, disappointments, confusion, and harm, and we go to a psychologist for assistance, most people try to rebuild the foundation they created that suddenly fell apart. When we do this it is important to remember that this new foundation will fall apart again. All that is man-made must crumble. A true foundation that never will crumble can only be found in the deepest recesses of life.

Going on a pilgrimage means letting the pieces of our lives lie all around us when they fall—not jumping in to rebuild them again, seeking man-made security. Going on a pilgrimage means not being so quick to judge another person, not placing others and ourselves in comfortable pigeonholes, so we know how to relate predictably. There is nothing comfortable or predictable on a pilgrimage. Here we endure discomfort gladly. We do not carry much baggage either, in case of an emergency. Other baggage such as resentments, grudges, old memories are also left behind us; if not, they weigh us down. It is brave to relinquish our hatred of others, but that is what pilgrimage demands. As we do this, all kinds of doors open, letting the fresh spring breeze in.

The Man on the Roof

A Zen student, Nava, lived in an apartment with a kitchen that looked out over the roof of a building a few doors down. For the past month, as she had her breakfast every morning, and looked out the window, she saw a man climb out of a trapdoor on the roof and pace around. He would go to the edge, lean over, look down, and then pull himself away and pace around the roof again. After doing this several times, he'd go back down the trapdoor to his apartment.

One morning as he stayed very close to the edge for a long time, leaning over, Nava became frightened, thinking he was close to suicide, and decided to call the police. She reported the man and his actions, but as he was unpredictable, came and went periodically, the police said there was nothing that could be done.

Nava went back to her morning coffee, gazing out at the desperate man. After about a month of this, one day he disappeared. No matter how long she waited for him, he did not climb out on the roof again.

Then, one day a few weeks later, Nava was stopped in her tracks as she was walking on the street. Walking a few steps beside her was the man from the rooftop. Despite herself she called out to him, "I'm so glad to see you. How are you?"

He turned and looked at her blankly.

"I saw you on the rooftop every morning from my window," she went on. "I was worried if you were all right."

He stopped cold and stared at her. "You were worried, huh?" he said.

"Yes. Are you okay? Were you thinking up there about jumping?"

He grinned. "I used to. I cared enough then."

"I'm sorry," said Nava.

"Bullshit. But I don't care anymore, either. Now when I go up on the roof, it's just for a smoke."

"I am sorry," Nava insisted.

"Oh yeah?" He looked at her strangely. "You care about what happens to me? But what's it worth? You didn't care enough to come over and climb out on the rooftop with me. You didn't come over and offer a hand."

> Wake up! Wake up!
> Then we'll become good friends
> sleeping butterfly.
>
> —*Basho*

Climbing Out on the Rooftop

Pilgrimage is climbing out on the rooftop with the stranger. Going from the safety of drinking coffee in a kitchen to being truly available, really extending a hand. Going out on the roof might seem a frightening or dangerous action; we have no idea what would happen. Perhaps he might even push us over with him. As the great teacher Hillel said, "If I'm not for myself who will be for me? But if I am only for myself, what am I?"

The only way of ending the torture of wanting the world, ourselves, and others to be safe and stable is to realize and accept that it is not. We must realize how to live in the midst of insecurity. Then we are living a life of pilgrimage.

On the Way

> One monk has left home but is not on the way,
> The other has never left home, but is on the way.
>
> —*Ancient Zen saying*

This is a well-known koan. Who are these monks? Of course each one is a part of ourselves. The koan comes to ask more deeply what is the way, and where is our true home? How do we relinquish that which is deadening, what is needed to be able to truly reach out to another, how do we truly become alive?

In Zen there is talk of leaving home, renunciation. Some take this to mean that they must leave their homes, families, jobs, friendships. This can be helpful for some, for a period of time, if they understand that it is for the purpose of practice, and that they will also create the very same families, homes, and friendships wherever they are going, unless they are willing to renounce their habits of mind and heart.

We can live life as a pilgrimage while remaining at home and with our families as well. All we must do then is renounce our usual, stale habits, thoughts, actions, and fears. We renounce the false security obtained from living life hiding in the kitchen, looking through the window. We renounce false security by recognizing that life is new and different each moment and that we cannot cling to outmoded responses that worked at another time and place. Renunciation of this kind means heading in a new direction each day, being willing to face the uniqueness of experience and discover something entirely different about others and ourselves. All moments of turning around, of letting go, of forgiveness are moments of pilgrimage, which take us from our hard-hearted ways to a land we have not yet known. In the Bible it is called the promised land.

THE PATH IN OUR HEARTS

The path is not somewhere in the sky,
It is in our hearts.

—*the Buddha*, The Dhammapada

The path of pilgrimage is waiting for us wherever we are, in all of our activities and relationships. Jane, a woman in her late fifties, called upon her friend, Lisa, a Zen student. Jane was nervous and sad.

"I'm being called to do something I'm horrified at," Jane said. "But I have to do it."

"What?" Lisa said.

"A dear friend of mine is dying," Jane continued. "She's been dying for a few years. Neither of us paid much attention to it. But the time is getting closer now. I haven't seen her for the past few months and now I hear she's really bad."

Lisa took a deep breath.

"She told another friend of ours," Jane continued, "that she wants me to visit now. She doesn't want to die without seeing me—she's waiting."

"Yes?" said Lisa.

"I'm terrified of doing this. I have no idea what to do or say. Help me figure out how to act. What happens if I cry?"

What happens if I cry? is a koan. Jane is terrified of being real. She is frightened of death, despair, loss, and the pain it brings. She's afraid of just being with her dying friend. She thinks who she is is not enough, that she must add something extra, figure out the right way to respond. There is no right way to respond when facing death. There is no greater way of bringing comfort to someone dying than simply being there with them wholeheartedly. Death is bigger than all games we play. What is wrong with shedding tears if they come? What is wrong with just holding a hand? What is wrong with who we are? Why do we so doubt the validity of our simple, spontaneous, authentic response?

Just like Nava's experience with the man on the rooftop, Jane is being called on a pilgrimage, away from her usual mode of being. This is a gift her dying friend is presenting. The friend also wants the simple gift of Jane's presence—that's all.

"Just go," Lisa answered. "Be there with her quietly, and let what happens, happen."

This is the essence of pilgrimage, faith in ourselves and in what is presented for us to do. We simply allow the situation to speak to us, accept the unpredictable, and from the depths of our heart, respond. The response that comes in this way is always fresh and new. In a sense we've climbed out of a window. Something unexpected can happen now. Musty rooms are suddenly filled with dew.

ZEN IN ACTION

Exercise 1: Find Your Own Pilgrimage

What constitutes a pilgrimage for you? Where are you stuck now? What do you cling to? Where is it you need to go? Write down your thoughts about pilgrimage. Have you ever been on one? Do you want to go?

Exercise 2: Renounce Old Habits

Today, renounce one habit that you normally cling to. Replace it with open space. Allow yourself to be available to whatever that habit closed off for you. Try another action or practice next week. And still another yet.

Exercise 3: A Fresh Start

Where are new, fresh responses needed in your life? List a few relationships that have gone dead. What are the pigeonholes you are placing them in? How do you view the other? How do you view yourself? Can you rid yourself and the other of the chains of the past? What happens when you do? Try this and see.

> There are those who can
> Abandon yesterday and tomorrow and today,
> Cross over to the farther shore
> Beyond life and death.
> Quiet your mind.
> Reflect
> Watch
> Nothing binds you.
> You are free.
>
> —*the Buddha*, The Dhammapada

PART FOUR

DISSOLVING THE FALSE SELF

CHAPTER 13

Putting Toys Away

When we are little we play with toys.
When we grow up we put our toys away and want the real thing.
—a Zen student

ZEN MIRACLE 13
We are no longer bored by our boredom.

Most of life is playing with toys. It's fun, enchanting, passes the time, and distracts us from one of our greatest fears—boredom. Nothing doing, being no one. When nothing is happening and we're bored we feel empty and dull. When there aren't distractions and entertainment, some people don't even know if they're really alive.

Many use their time and life force in finding respite from boredom. They search for new scenery, people, places, books, activities, friends. They tell others about their exciting vacations and adventures and feel as if they are where it's *really happening*— as if they're fully living their lives. They never ask what it is that's happening—or what it means to fully live one's life. They dread the time when they will be unable to "do things" and have to be silent, alone with themselves.

PLAYING WITH TOYS

When we play with toys we feel as though our lives have purpose. Wonderful fantasies usually accompany our play, and these fantasies provide energy and excitement. When a man is driving in a brand new red convertible with the top down, singing at the top of his lungs, he feels wild, free, full of possibilities, a guy most girls would love to have. He may imagine that others, looking at him from cars on the road, are envying his freedom. Suppose he were riding a motorcycle instead, zooming along at full speed, the wind in his hair, feeling freedom and power, and then the bike hits an oil slick, flips over, and throws him smack on the gravel, smashing his bones. What happens to his freedom then? Where is his power or sense of aliveness? Was his moment of exhilaration true freedom and power? Fantasies can be dangerous friends.

When our toys are worn out, or break in half, we immediately grab for new ones to play with. If we do not do this, but stay fully awake in that moment, able to tolerate what may feel like loss, emptiness, or boredom, a new understanding of freedom arises, one that cannot be broken, that is not dependent upon anything.

In Zen we call these fantasies that fuel our lives *delusions*. They are considered one of the three poisons (the others are greed and anger)—actually the hardest one to detect. We have delusions about everything, who we are, who the other person is, what we are doing, where we are going, and the outcome of all our deeds.

OUR TRUE LIFE

The great Zen Master Dogen says:

> If fish are taken out of water they will not live. Water is life for fish, air is life for birds.

> What is life for man? Are these fantasies and toys our true life? If they are, as we grow, why do we crave that which is real?

Fantasies creep upon us skillfully, so we do not know they are even there. They are like imaginary flowers dancing in front of our eyes. Unfortunately, while some of these flowers are beautiful, others are simply weeds. Whether they are weeds or beautiful blossoms, delusions or fantasies, they obstruct our view. They do not provide a clear picture of our lives or those in it. No matter how happy or excited we become, actions based upon delusions are off base. They do not lead to where we think we are going, nor do they provide the returns we so long for.

Imaginary Flowers in the Sky

A brother and two sisters who hadn't seen each other for some time met for a quick lunch. One of the sisters had to move and the three of them planned to eat quickly before going together to look at a community she was interested in. They met at a local luncheonette, ordered sandwiches and, happy to see one another, began reminiscing about past days. As soon as lunch was over they planned to head to Riverdale, about half an hour away, but as they sat there reminiscing, thinking of days that had gone by, other ideas came to mind.

"I don't think Riverdale's the right place," the brother said out of the blue. "Remember how you always loved the ocean? You should go back there to live now. How about trying Bay Ridge, Brooklyn?"

"Bay Ridge," one sister crooned. "He's right. It feels better. Salty breezes, long walks at the ocean."

None of them knew Bay Ridge very well, or had any idea how to get there.

"No," the other sister chirped in, "when you mention Brooklyn, I think of Park Slope. Just the sound of it—Park Slope."

"Park Slope's the place for you," the cheerful brother excitedly replied. "I've heard wonderful things about it—winding streets, friendly faces. Must have a beautiful park. Imagine how the trees look in the autumn with winding bicycle paths."

Of course he'd never been there either. As the time passed the three of them were gripped with fantasies about places, one image replacing the next. Fantasy built upon fantasy, and before they knew it, it was much later—almost time for evening rush hour.

"No point in going anywhere now. We'll hit terrible traffic," said the one who had to go in the first place. "May as well stay where we are and order more dessert."

This is exactly the way fantasies affect us. They can grab us, grip us, immobilize us, present amazing pictures (which usually have very little to do with reality), and either stop constructive action, or prompt us to take actions that lead into a maze.

The sisters and brother were bathed in their fantasies. Their confusion about where to go was not based upon this Zen teaching.

Going somewhere doesn't take you anyplace else.
                                        —*Ancient Zen saying*

This quote refers to the fact that we take our fantasies with us wherever we go, and asks us to find the place where we are truly at home.

The Basis of Delusion

What is the basis of delusion, of feeling we must run here and there seeking our good? What keeps it so rooted in our lives? Why do we cling to it so tenaciously?

The sense that what is in front of my eyes is real, that there is something I lack and must find in this world is the nature of all delusion. This kind of misunderstanding comes from not knowing who I really am, what life is, and what I am doing here. It is a yearning to become someone important, to make life seem worthwhile.

This craving is, of course, based upon the feeling that I am not someone important already, that life, as it is, is not worthwhile. This craving implies that it is up to me to "make myself" into someone, that who I am now is not full and complete. It denies my intrinsic Buddha Nature.

Buddha Nature exists within us forever. It cannot be created by us, just found, lived from, realized. The way we realize it, in Zen practice, is to eliminate, to pay no attention to the delusions about ourselves that we foster. We ignore the persistent feeling that we are insufficient, that we must become something or someone else.

As we experience boredom, just sitting doing nothing, letting dreams come and go, seeing them for what they are, simply illusions with no basis, our self-created identity, or ego, dissolves. Sitting there in that manner we become nothing, with nothing to do, nothing to think, nowhere to go. Our social identity is vacated. Our dreams of ourselves have no place to stick. Although painful to many, this is an excellent first step for reaching the palace where our true selves reside.

> All of man's troubles and anguish arises from his being unable
> to be alone with himself in a room, with nothing to do.
> —*Franz Kafka*

REALIZING BUDDHA NATURE

In order to realize and live from our Buddha Nature, we must first realize that the life we are living is false, filled with toys that do not provide the sense of meaning we long for. It is a life of hypnosis, addiction, and slavery to the outside world, a life dominated by dreams, fluctuations, illness, and loss. Truly we are living our precious lives caught inside of a mirage. As we search for lasting happiness and peace, through the tangles of everyday experience, sooner or later, we grow disillusioned and weary. Our search seems to bear no fruit. But this is not entirely so. Like boredom, disillusionment is a wonderful experience, a necessary step before we are ready to plant our two feet firmly on the earth.

It is absolutely necessary to be able to tolerate boredom, or what feels like a lack of stimulation or emptiness. This emptiness we feel initially is not the true emptiness, but the silence and simplicity we live our lives so frightened of. It is simply the relinquishing of delusions and the false excitement they generate.

A famous koan that relates to the question of the world of delusion and practice is:

"A monk said to Ummon—'The world is vast and wide—why do we put on our robes at the sound of the bell?'"

The world is vast and wide, so many pleasures, so many wonderful things to do. Why do we stop at the sound of the bell, put on our robes, and sit on a cushion? Why are we exchanging rigor and boredom for so-called freedom? Why are we tasting the bitter as well as the sweet? Are we running away, leaving the world? Where *is* this world that is vast and wide? How do we really enjoy it?

WHAT'S THE CASE?

When a Zen student, Maya, was asked to give a talk at a sesshin, the head monk wanted to know what koan she would be talking about.

"What's the case?" he asked.

"I'm the case," she said.

We are all the case. Our own lives are the case. Our koans are given to us every day. Part of the wonderful medicine of this practice is to find the truth in everything that happens.

Our practice is not about somebody else. Our koans are not about men in the old days. Here we recover our own lives, take ourselves back from enchantment, from the many spells we have been placed under and put ourselves under day by day. To do this it is necessary to be willing to see delusions as the bubbles they are, which, although beautiful, must burst eventually. We have to understand what is medicine and what is poison.

As we discard our illusions, put our toys away, what are we left with? What kind of life do we have?

Zen is the simple life of eating your rice and then washing your bowl.

—*Ancient Zen saying*

For many, the simple, plain life, the life of eating rice and washing your bowl seems like a life of boredom, but in truth this is a life to be greatly prized. It is a life filled with appropriate action, taken at the perfect moment. But how many are in harmony with nature, their bodies, and their true needs? Most lives are not governed by natural rhythms. They are governed by delusions and wild imaginings. They are governed by destructive injunctions created by society, such as "thin is beautiful, fat is ugly." I must be thin and beautiful, no matter what my body is saying to me. I will not eat this morning, I'll run until I drop to lose this weight. This person never begins to discover the natural beauty and true body they live from each day. When they do, hunger takes its rightful place, they eat what is correct for that day.

Finding Our Natural Body

We all have our natural body, our intrinsic body of true needs and feelings. A great mistake many make when they speak of Zen is to think that this practice turns us into zombies or robots, that the practitioner "transcends" the physical world. Nothing can be further from the truth. This practice helps us enter our bodies and live fully in the world. It places us directly in accord with our natural rhythms.

Living from fantasy and delusion does the opposite. It makes it impossible for us to hear, feel, and know the truth of our lives as we live it, moment by moment. It makes us susceptible to manipulation and the need to live out the fantasies of others. A life such as this is never rewarding. At the end the individual wonders where his precious years went, what happened to his energy, what he has left at the end.

The arrow shot, spent, falls down and returns to earth again.

—*Ancient Zen saying*

The arrow is our life—once spent, once scattered in toys and dreams, it falls back down, exhausted, returning to the earth once again. In order to find our natural body, or true nature as it is called, we embark upon this lifelong practice to empty ourselves not of natural needs, but of false desires and appetites.

ZEN IN ACTION

Exercise 1: Allow Boredom

Write down three activities that bore you completely. Then do one a day. Do it for as long as you can bear. Experience this boredom fully.

Exercise 2: Enjoy Daydreams

Write down your favorite fantasies, daydreams, and delusions, the ones you run to when things get particularly rough. Write them down in great detail. Sit there and enjoy them. Decide that for fifteen minutes each day you will do nothing but daydream and fantasize. After those fifteen minutes are over, let the daydreams go.

If you find yourself fantasizing at other times, be aware that you are doing this. Interrupt these persistent delusions by simply noting you're daydreaming again. Doing this on an ongoing basis will begin to take their steam away; they will lose their grip over you. You may be surprised to realize how delusions creep up and grab your most precious possessions—your life force and attention. Your time and attention are precious resources. Do not allow your delusions to steal them from you.

Exercise 3: Give Away Toys

Find something that has been a toy for you that you can part with now. Give it away. See what it's like to be without it, what else appears in its place.

Now, do that with another toy when you're ready. Give them away, one at a time. Notice how you are feeling, and what your life is without them.

CASE 37: (FROM *MUMONKAN*— TRANSLATED FROM *THE GATELESS GATE*)

Koan: *Joshu's Oak Tree*

A monk asked Joshu, "What is the meaning of Bodidharma's coming to China?"

Joshu said, "The oak tree in the garden."

MUMON'S COMMENT

If you understand Joshu's answer intimately, there is no Shakya before you, no Buddha of the future to come.

MUMON'S VERSE

Words cannot express things;
Speech does not convey the spirit.
Swayed by words, one is lost;
Blocked by phrases, one is bewildered.

The oak tree in the garden stands in all its grandeur. Once you see it, dreams fade away.

CHAPTER 14

When Medicine Turns to Poison

ZEN MIRACLE 14
*We can tell the difference
between poison and medicine.*

> The whole world is medicine
> What is the illness?
> —*Ancient Zen saying*

When Medicine Turns into Poison

We live in the world not knowing what is medicine and what is poison (or delusions). We don't know what we really need, what will make us strong, healthy, clear, and compassionate, and what will cause a lot of anguish. So what we have is a great deal of confusion. We think if we like something, if it tastes good and goes down nicely, that it is going to be good for us. If we like a person, if they're sweet, kind, charming, it's medicine. We want to run to that kind of person, food, or experience. We go to whatever tastes sweet and delicious. Then things suddenly change and we become dismayed, so we come to a therapist and say, "It started out so

161

wonderfully. He was so sweet, kind, charming in the beginning. Now it's a mess. How come I was betrayed?"

Of course we are never betrayed by a person, only by our own false expectations. In fact, when a person is in a relationship that seems so sweet and lovely, where everything they want is being supplied, this person may not understand why they are feeling worse, becoming weaker and more dependent, or increasingly frightened that the partner will go away. If the situation is weakening you, it's poison.

On the other side, we can become involved with people and situations that are terrifically bitter, that we don't like. These are painful and we want to run away. Some people in these situations come to therapists asking, "Why can't I be in a relationship where things are normal and healthy? How come I'm always being yelled at? I don't deserve treatment like that. I'm getting out of here."

BUILDING SELF-WORTH

Most therapists will agree that their patients don't deserve bitter treatment. From a psychological point of view, sifting medicine from poison means finding relationships and circumstances that are positive and feel constructive to the self. This means that they meet the individual's personal needs and enhance their sense of self-worth. While, on the one hand, of course, this is desirable, there is also a danger of building up false ego and pride, making a person feel that his or her whole world revolves around receiving his or her needs, separating an individual from his or her true worth. What is implicit and not examined is that the individual's sense of personal value in these cases comes from being treated properly by someone else, receiving respect. They feel good about themselves when they have "sweet" experiences in life, achieve their goals, win the love they desire. And when they don't, or when they lose the love they cherish—then what?

These relationships that feel like medicine can be poison if they develop a sense of false pride, catering to a bloated, demanding personality who will only be satisfied by what he or she wants, and who uses others as instruments to attain its desires.

The deeper question of *who* it is that craves this respect, may go unattended to. The awareness that there is a larger Self within us may become drowned out.

Zen practice works differently. It dissolves false ego and pride so that the Buddha Nature can appear.

DON'T YELL AT ME

A Zen student, Maya, particularly hated to be yelled at. She would do anything to avoid it. So, of course, when she started practice she was constantly yelled at by her teacher. Whatever she did, he yelled at her for it and she cried. Then he would yell again. Finally it became a joke. If three people were talking, the teacher would only hear Maya, stop the conversation and confront her about it. When this happened often enough it finally didn't mean so much anymore. His yelling became like a thunderstorm, not something personal directed at her. It was like a cold wind coming from the north. When Maya felt at home with the yelling, it stopped.

At first she thought, *This yelling is poison, who needs to be around something so hard and painful?* This is like when we sit on the cushion and it hurts so much; then we get up to leave and we wonder why we feel so strong, so much more in command of our lives.

STUCK IN HONEY

When we only run to things and people that taste and feel good, we get stuck in honey like bees. The addiction to this sweetness in life can trap us, often we can't get out. In that case the sweetness turns into a different kind of poison.

Mulla Nasrudin, in the Sufi tradition, was sitting, eating hot peppers, and crying because each one was bitter. Then he ate the next one and it was more bitter, then the next one. He hated it.

They said to him, "Why are you eating all these hot peppers?" He said, "I'm waiting for a sweet one."

That's like us, waiting for a sweet one—a sweet sitting, a person, a situation. We're waiting for the goodness, not realizing the bitterness itself can be good. In Zen practice we do not sit and wait for a sweet chili pepper; we realize these are all hot peppers and stop longing for a sweet one. Normally, we are always dissatisfied with whatever we're given, with where we are, with the people we meet. People are always complaining, "Oh, he's not tall enough, not smart enough, too restless, only comes to visit for three hours a month and then disappears." We're waiting for the person or situation to be right, so we, too, can feel important.

Zen practice says to become completely at home with the bitter and sweet (because that is what you, too, are). Taste both thoroughly, and don't get indigestion. We get such indigestion with our experience we can never swallow anything. We judge it, hate it, we won't chew it up and take it down. Zazen is the process of chewing up our experience, whatever it is, tasting it, and swallowing it. Very difficult, painful, and strengthening. As we do this, we may find, to our surprise, that what we thought was poison (what was hurtful and frightening) is really medicine. Somehow, it is making us well.

A Fire in the Kitchen

Maya called Sara, another Zen student, and said, "Guess what happened? Even though I've been quite sick for some time with terrible pain in my back, I made this holiday meal at my house."

Sara said, "Yes?"

"Well, during the meal there was a fire in the kitchen—grease splattered the floor, someone got burnt, and I fell flat on my back."

Sara was startled. She said, "A fire in your kitchen? Why?"

A fire in the kitchen, why? is another kind of koan. Everyone wants to know *why*, but this particular fire is a story about how medicine turns to poison, and the other way around.

Maya prepared this holiday meal while ill, with lots of pain in her back. When it came time for serving the food, due to her painful back, one of her sons had to go to the kitchen and pull out the large pot out of the oven. It was heavy, and as he was pulling it, it slipped and hot grease splattered out, spilled onto the oven door, the floor and over his legs. Flames were spitting out of the oven as he yelled, "I'm scalded. Help!"

In horror Maya jumped up. She ran into the kitchen, not realizing grease was all over the floor. The minute she got there, her feet went out from under her, and she fell down—whack!—right on her back. Shocked, she lay absolutely still, like a dead woman.

Alex, another guest at the meal, ran in after her and cried out, "She's dead."

Her brother banged on the table and said, "This is a holiday from hell."

In total disarray everyone rushed into the kitchen to help. The brother didn't move from his seat, but continued to sit there eating, terrified about what would happen next.

As Maya, in shock, still hadn't moved, Alex stood there calling out, "It's over. She's dead."

Maya perked up and called back, "I'm alive."

As she lay there, naturally she started wondering, *Why is this happening to me? What did I do wrong? Am I being punished with a fire on this holiday?*

Despite her troubled thoughts the fire went out by itself, the son's burns were easily soothed, and soon time came for her to get up. When she did she was shaky, but the pain in her back had vanished. It became pain somewhere else, on the bottom of her spine. That was sore, but didn't hurt as much. All the awful pain had disappeared.

Another guest, Francine, a delicate woman, didn't say anything. She was horrified by all that went on. Francine had an exceptionally strong dislike of mess and housework and always had someone at home cleaning for her. When she got up and peered into the kitchen, she wanted to gag. The grease was splattered everywhere and everyone had to pitch in. Francine was handed wet cloths and a mop and asked to wipe up the greasy floor.

Each guest had received whatever they feared or hated. Maya was hit on her back, Francine had to clean up the floor, the son, who had a fear of fire, got burnt. Medicine or poison? Of course, our first reaction to this kind of circumstance is to seek an explanation, to ask why it happened.

The thinking mind starts to explain and make up reasons right away. Eventually we are lost in a fog of explanations, many of which cause more pain than the original injury. The beautiful thing about falling down hard is that it stops all this thinking, cold. Bang—whack! Maya was just there with the experience, 100 percent. When this happened, not only did her thoughts vanish, but the pain went with them. When she stood up she was fine.

How do we know what is going to be the healing? In Zen practice we do not begin spinning answers, but just take the blow—bang! Not fighting back, not hating anyone, including oneself. Practice is just to take the whack. Pain comes, okay. Joy comes, good. We do not push one away, or pull another to us. It's presumptuous to think we always know which is which.

The only way to arrive at a healing solution to our life, to put the toys away, is to be willing to take our experience and say "thank you" for whatever comes. In the Lotus Sutra it says, "Only turn away from what is false and you will find what is true." But just to be able to know what is false and what is true takes much practice.

As we turn away from what is false, that which is true will appear by itself. We may have to wait for the truth and not accept half-truths or lies as the truth. We know when we are in a moment of truth. Our bones, cells, heart know it. We know when we are sitting in a moment of compassion for another person. Just to know what is poison and what is medicine is not so easy. Sometimes what looks like part of the cure is part of the sickness.

We know it's medicine and not poison by the presence of love, of compassion, of joy, of fun. But remember, poison turns to medicine constantly and medicine turns to poison. One isn't bad and the other good. Without poison we have no medicine. And without medicine, no poison. They go back and forth. If we're sitting in a moment of poison, that itself is the medicine.

Here is a poem by Rumi about this. His word for love and ours for compassion, oneness, or awakeness are the same.

> Through love all that is bitter will be sweet.
> Through love all that is copper will be gold.
> Through love all dregs will turn into the purest wine.
> Through love all pain will turn into medicine.
>
> —*Rumi*

GREAT LAUGHTER

> Years searching on the edge of the mountain, now great laughter at the bottom of the lake.
>
> —*Ancient Zen saying*

After the dinner, as Maya realized that she was well, she broke into great laughter. What's the joke? What is this great laughter? Why is it so hard to come by? Why is the sound of this great laughter the most wonderful medicine of all?

Great laughter also means great freedom, and great enjoyment with everything. We have finally stopped seeking and are able to taste, receive, and appreciate whatever is given. What a wonderful way to say "thank you" for the miracle of being alive. Until we have great laughter, we may still be fighting the world off, hiding from it in our fantasies, or trying to make it something it is not, caught up in constructing endless interpretations and meanings about whatever we are up against.

We have lived believing that there is something wrong with this incredible universe that presents itself daily before our eyes, that life itself, as it arises, is not sufficient. This has driven us completely crazy. We believe it is up to us to control all conditions, events, and people we encounter. We have run to therapists, doctors, and psychiatrists, who are stuck in the same dilemma. We run everywhere searching for our true healing or life.

Life is life to man. If you separate yourself from life, you, too, will die. If you live out of dreams, demands, and delusions you are separating yourself from life and will live out your time as a ghost. This means you live your life as a false man, always battling or resisting this or that. You will hate pain and only cling to pleasure, hate the bad one and only love the good. You will never come truly alive or understand the saying:

Nirvana is Samsara—Samsara is Nirvana.

—Ancient Zen saying

This Very Life Is Heaven

Samsara is the phenomenal world, our daily lives, with all the repetitive struggles, conflicts, yearnings, joys, and disappointments. Nirvana is considered to be a place of peace, equanimity, a place free from continual ups and downs. Most feel that to have ultimate peace or equanimity, they must somehow reject their lives or samsara, escape from or control the phenomenal world. Some go permanently to mountains to meditate, others identify only with certain small groups and reject everyone else. Confusion and fury grow uncontrollably, fueled by delusions and self-righteousness.

Zen practice puts an end to that. *Nirvana Is Samsara* means the phenomenal world, everyday life, is the place where true peace dwells, no one and nothing excluded. Enter real life and live it fully. Do not separate yourself.

When I, a student of Dharma
Look at the real form of the universe,
All is the never-failing manifestation
Of the mysterious truth.

In any event, in any moment,
And in any place,
None can be other than the marvelous revelation
Of its glorious light.

     —*Torei Zenji*, Bodhisattva's Vow

ZEN IN ACTION

Exercise 1: What Is the Sickness?

What is something in your personal life that you would consider sickness? How are you treating it? What medicine are you taking? What is the sickness it is seeking to cure? Think about that harder. Look at the sickness again. And again. Now once again, look at the medicine. See if you can see it all differently. Is there another way of holding the sickness, another way of finding a cure?

Exercise 2: No More Resisting

Find something you are resisting deeply. Just sit still with it. Welcome it. Embrace it deeply. Allow yourself to resist. Resist more now. Let that be perfectly all right. Allow yourself to allow it to actually disappear from your life. After an amount of time passes, look at it once again. When we stop resisting resistance, something new can take place. (You may no longer want or need it. Or, it may seem easier to approach.)

Exercise 3: Life Is Life for Man

Where are you looking for your life? What makes you feel most alive? What is life to you? Ponder these questions and enjoy them.

  Now today, moment by moment, realize that each person and event that happens is life for you. Life is not somewhere else. See how fully you can accept the life that presents itself to you now.

CASE 87: (FROM *HEKIGANROKU*—
TRANSLATED FROM
THE BLUE CLIFF RECORDS)

Koan: Medicine and Sickness Cure Each Other

Ummon said to his disciples, "Medicine and sickness cure each other. All the earth is medicine. Where do you find yourself?"

SETCHO'S VERSE
> All the earth is medicine;
> Ancient and modern, men make a great mistake.
> Shut the gate, but do not build the cart;
> The universe is the highway, vast and wide.
> Mistaken, all is mistaken.
> Though their noses are stuck up to heaven,
> They will still be pierced for a rope.

CHAPTER 15

THE TRUE MAN OF NO RANK

ZEN MIRACLE 15
We can become a doorman.

From the High Seat, the Master said, "Up on the lump of red flesh there is a True Man of No Rank who ceaselessly goes out and in through the gates of your face. Those who have not yet recognized him, look out, look out!"

A monk came forward and asked, "What is the True Man of No Rank?"

The Master descended from his seat, grabbed the monk and said, "Speak! Speak!"

The monk hesitated.

The Master released him and said, "What a shit-stick is this True Man of No Rank is!" Then he withdrew to his quarters.

—Rinzai

This fierce and relentless story contains the essence, taste and quest of Zen practice—to find *the true man of no rank*, and once found, to express his life vividly. Hesitation will not do. Imitation is scoffed at. Sweet words which cover up, are despised. False piety and kindness are stepped on. The true man of no rank does not pretend to be a holy saint. He is the quintessence of humility. However, when he hesitates, relapses back to his false, stumbling self, Rinzai calls him a shit-stick.

This shit-stick itself is a koan. Please remember a shit-stick (or toilet paper) is no better or worse than anything else. It, too, contains precious Buddha Nature. All of life joins in this practice, nothing is left out.

THE INSANE EGO

The shit-stick is used to wake students up, to break the power of the insane false ego. Once false ego and pride are dissolved, the true man of no rank can finally live his life free from encumbrances. Ultimately, to live a life apart from our true man (or woman) of no rank is more than most of us can bear.

The treatment the Master dished out to his disciple may sound too rough, cruel, or crude. None of this is really so. In fact, in Zen, it is thought that the Master used all of his considerable strength to wake his student up. He even showed grandmotherly kindness to him.

The urgency of the task before us, the danger of living ensconced in lies, is so great, that strong methods must be taken. Time is of the essence. Not a moment can be wasted. Everything becomes an opportunity to awaken. If a true teacher is present he is continually vigilant to find the right moment to free the student. When the disease is advanced, the medicine must be potent. Most Zen Masters live by the following axiom:

> The great need before our eyes does not allow us to go by the rules.
>
> —*Book of the Zen Grove*

An older woman, Marsha, had been in a relationship with an older man for about twenty years, and though they never married he loved her very much. Despite that, she constantly feared that he would leave her one day when she got older and go after a younger woman. Secretly she believed he'd finally have the child he never had. As the years passed this became an obsession for her, so that wherever they went, whatever they did, she became more and more convinced this was about to happen. Naturally, this spoiled whatever they were doing, what lovely time they could be having.

One spring they went on vacation to the beach and were given a room with a patio on the ocean. As luck would have it, the patio next to them was taken by an older man with a younger woman, with a little baby. So, here was the entire picture of what she most feared.

It is not unusual to attract what one fears the most, and there they were, stuck on the beach next to this patio. Marsha's boyfriend started looking at the family saying, "Wow, look at that. He has such a young woman."

From that point on the vacation was over for Marsha. She was devastated, couldn't sleep, didn't want to eat, felt as if her world fell apart.

"I was nothing anymore at that moment," she said. "My youthful energy, my beauty, my entire value as a person was struck from me."

The next day as they were sitting on the beach the couple arrived with the little child and Marsha began to have terrible feelings about all of them. So much hate arose, it frightened her. There she was on a beautiful vacation with the sun shining and she was sitting there filled with fear and hatred.

Soon, however, she began to speak to these people and found out that they were not boyfriend and girlfriend, but father and daughter. "Ah," she said, and in that moment, she began to love the beautiful child. A few moments later she realized that aside from his daughter, the other older man was without a companion. How refreshing, she thought, now her boyfriend could realize that older men are often left alone. Then she thought she noticed this single man looking at her with admiration. Jubilant, she now felt beautiful, totally on top of the world. The whole night before she was up in agony; now she was sitting on the beach filled with delight.

These are the machinations of the false ego and pride. One moment filled with hate for this child for no reason, the next moment on the top of the world, because the circumstances look different and the ego feels loveable again.

Zazen combats this intense affliction by continually becoming aware of the difference between fantasy and reality, between looking at who we are really and what we're dreaming up.

From the psychological viewpoint, Marsha had been projecting her fears and dreams out upon the world and the people on the beach. Psychologically speaking, projection is also seen as a dangerous phenomenon which leads to convoluted relationships, living in the past, not knowing what's really going on. An excess of projection leads to paranoia, and loss of reality testing.

The true man of no rank is one who has no need to project anything. He is a clear mirror, simply viewing what is there, offering compassion and light to whatever comes.

BEING THE TRUTH

Because it encouraged righteous pride and ego the Buddha himself rejected the religious institutions and hierarchies of his day. He rejected external authority and set out upon a quest not only to find, but to *be* the truth. When we *are* the truth, the split between what we know and who we are vanishes. We do not speak and think one way and act another. We manifest what is true.

The greatest psychological pain we all suffer is the pain of being split, false, conflicted. This comes from knowing one thing, and being, or living, another. Knowledge that has not been digested, absorbed into our very bones, becomes poison that we carry like cancer. That is why the emphasis in Zen is not upon knowing, but being. It is not what you know, but who you are, that speaks volumes. In the story about Master Rinzai and the monk, the monk hesitated. His answer had not become his very life itself. He had to stop and think. He failed. The Zen Master got down and left quickly. The Zen Master's reaction was a manifestation of truth. His direct action spoke loudly. Zen practice banishes external knowledge so the student can live from the truth of himself.

The Zen man knows where his treasure lies. He will avoid fruitless argument and discussion. When the time arrives he will help others without seeking for himself. He realizes others are himself. When others are wrong, he is wrong.

WHEN OTHERS ARE WRONG, I AM WRONG

Many spiritual practices are based upon defining who and what is right and wrong. (Usually one's particular practice is right and all others, wrong.) Practitioners in this mode easily become self-righteous, seeing the whole world as sinners and themselves as saints. Half the world must be changed and reformed. In Zen this is seen as the height of arrogance. Who are we to sit in judgment upon the incredible creation in front of our eyes? How is it possible for so-called religious men and women to claim to love God and yet reject huge parts of Creation?

In Zen we say, "When others are wrong, I am wrong." This is the antithesis of arrogance. I am wrong for viewing others as wrong. Also, as I am others, if they are wrong, I must correct the error in myself as well. I do not praise myself and blame others. All negativity placed upon others is clearly seen to be simply negativity in my own mind. Zazen breaks through the projectivity of the human mind. It points clearly to the fact that we project out upon the world what it is we feel, hate, or long for within. Better to take the projections back, to see where these images come from. What is the source of these projections?

Look at Your Own Deeds, Done and Undone

As we engage in Zen practice, we pull our attention forcefully away from its constant preoccupation with the faults and deeds of others and look deeply at ourselves. It is our own actions we account for. This is where the emphasis lies. The response of others to our behavior becomes of little consequence.

We learn not to long for praise, or retreat from censure. A Zen Master will censure his student mercilessly. Although this looks cruel, it can be kind. The student is learning not to depend upon external praise or kindness, which is, at best, fleeting and vain. The student is learning not to use his actions to build up a false sense of self. This kind of treatment from the Master helps the student relinquish the false masks he hides behind. The more disappointment he endures, the less his manipulations bear fruit, the quicker he will relinquish them, go within and find his true strength.

Take the Mask Off

Many come to practice enclosed in layers of games and masks and then yearn to understand the true nature of suffering. But how can we be anything but lonely and cut off if we live behind a false persona, always trying to be something we're not? How can we do anything but suffocate?

> When you become real, life becomes real. When you become you, Zen becomes Zen.
>
> —*Ancient Zen saying*

As soon as the mask comes off, the glittering light shines through. Life is fresh, constantly renewed, and we are, too. These masks may not be so not easy to take off, though. Even if they constrict us at every turn, we'll fight to the death to keep them on. We think they are our security and beauty; without them we feel naked and bare. Some become so accustomed to wearing these masks that they confuse them with their very own skin.

Throughout most of our lives we play a variation of the game of Let's Pretend. Let's pretend that you are King Arthur and I am the Queen. Let's pretend that you didn't say that and I didn't hear. Let's pretend it all doesn't matter. I help you keep your pretenses up and you help me keep up mine. In one way this makes us feel safe and secure. In another, it robs our true life from us. We live in a make-believe world and become cardboard people. If someone knocks on our door to visit, most of the time there's no one home.

When we live our lives presenting fronts to others, we lose touch with who we truly are. When we retreat into roles and games the words we say will be empty. People will listen and not believe. Our sense of trust is impaired. Only when we are able to put our games, masks, and roles aside, will true presence and love arise.

Everyone fears being exposed. Some would rather die than have their masks taken off. Even many of those who are quite ill are still primarily concerned about how they look to others and the impression they will make.

But as we grow older in life, the changes we encounter wipe out all images and eventually take away the masks and games. Who are we, then, when our pretenses are gone? What is it we are so afraid of exposing? Why is the true man of no rank so hard to find and to live from day by day?

We cling to masks and roles the way a drowning man clings to a lifeboat. If someone questions or insults the masks we hold, we feel as though we are dying inside. Some would kill to uphold their public image. Some kill themselves when this image is gone.

Zen practice knows that these images are the very cause of our pain, and that we must break out of our self-encased shells, the way a chick pecks continually from inside its shell, desperate to come out and be born.

A Zen student, Jeffrey, kept returning to dokusan with the same koan. Whatever answer he brought was dismissed by the Master. This went on for two years. Finally, in desperation, Jeffrey yelled out,

"What should I do to answer? Tell me!"
"Come naked before me," the Zen Master replied.

COME NAKED BEFORE ME

The Zen Master did not mean for Jeffrey to become physically naked. Zen practice is about being born. All dokusan, all private meetings with the Master, are simply for the purpose of becoming naked, and meeting the Master face to face. A true meeting. Nothing in between. Words then become unnecessary. When Martin Buber said, "All real living is meeting," it was this kind of meeting he was referring to.

The minute you walk into dokusan (the private meeting with the Master), he sees whether you are truly there. If you are not, he rings the bell to dismiss you. You dare not waste his precious time. When Rinzai got down from his seat and walked away, he was dismissing the monk who wasn't really there.

If you walk in as a ghost, seeking false comfort or answers, you must be dismissed immediately! Searching for false answers or comfort is not neutral. It is part of the poison that takes our true life away.

> There have to be real people before there is real knowledge.
> —*Ancient Zen saying*

It can take years and years to become ready for a real meeting, or it can happen suddenly. Zen practice itself may be thought of as the process of becoming ready. In order to become available to such a meeting, of course, our ego and pride must be dissolved.

HOW TO BE A DOORMAN

At a large conference on religion, morning zazen was offered as one of the many workshops available. The zazen meeting was assigned to a room in the basement near the cafeteria. Two large doors opened to a hallway outside the room. A wheelchair ramp extended from one of the doors. Though the zazen meeting was scheduled from six to seven in the morning, and a sign on the outside of the door said ZAZEN MEETING—QUIET PLEASE, other people started gathering outside in the hallway long before it was over, eager to pass through on their way to breakfast in the cafeteria. The participants in the Zen workshop could hear the crowd gather as they were doing zazen.

Not only did the crowd chatter loudly, but they kept opening the door to the room and peeking in. One person was extremely upset that the doors were closed and began knocking loudly on the door at a quarter to seven. Needless to say, this not only disrupted the atmosphere, but created a sense of chaos outside.

The leader of the zazen workshop tried to get the room changed, but it was impossible. The zazen meeting was not considered important, just a form of morning relaxation or exercise. The other rooms were reserved for important theological discussions, like grace, faith, prayer, and receiving the presence of God.

The leader then turned to the twenty participants who were sitting and asked if they would be willing to take turns being "doorman"—standing at the door, making sure the people outside were quiet, and that the door was not continually opened. This became a vital function as someone had to assume to preserve the atmosphere of the zazen meeting.

No one volunteered. No one wished to give up their time "meditating" to do something so unimportant as being a doorman. After all, they argued, they paid for the conference and wanted to get their full money's worth. They wanted to go home knowing how to do zazen, not how to be a doorman. They didn't understand that true zazen and being a doorman were precisely the same thing.

The conference was scheduled to go on for five days. The leader asked other officials at the conference if someone, somewhere, would volunteer to be "doorman" for an hour in the morning. Again, no one was willing to do so.

Every day before the zazen was over the agitated banging on the door started earlier, and became more insistent. Finally, on the fourth day, a man in a wheelchair burst through the doors, yelling and screaming that they had no right to keep the doors closed— he was hungry and had no other way to get through the campus.

As he wheeled into the room and saw others sitting in silence, he grew even more agitated, railing against the idiocy. Then he grabbed a huge garbage can that was standing in his path and hurled it at the sitters.

The stunned leader jumped up, grabbed the can, and pushed it out of the way.

"I'm so sorry," she exclaimed, "but you don't understand. I couldn't find anyone to be doorman."

The man in the wheelchair spluttered, and slowed down. "What are you talking about?"

He and the leader stared at each other. Her apology stopped him in his tracks. She had had no idea there had been a man in a wheelchair out there. He had no idea about her, either, what she was doing, or what she needed.

"Would you like to be our doorman?" she asked breathlessly.

The man in the wheelchair grew silent, then suddenly began to cry. He nodded his head. "Why didn't you ask me sooner?"

"I didn't realize."

"I'd love to," he said.

He arrived very early the next morning and stood guard outside the door. The last day was quiet, settled, and beautiful.

After the participants in the workshop left, the man in the wheelchair stayed behind.

"Thank you for teaching me about Zen," he said.

"Thank you for teaching me," she replied.

The two of them left the meeting room together.

"If you come back next year, I'll be the doorman," he said.

"Thank you so much," she said.

No one wants to be a doorman. Everyone wants the peace and bliss they think meditation can bring. True peace and contentment come only when you are ready to be a doorman, take the least job, be there for others, not think of yourself. Then you become everyone. Your personal needs disappear.

> The process of freeing yourself from arrogance and cutting off your habitual tendencies is a very drastic measure—but it is necessary in order to help others in this world.
>
> —*Trungpa*

Freeing Oneself from Arrogance

We live our lives ensconced in arrogance that is totally unmerited. The meditators in the story above thought they were doing something wonderful and holy. They were not. They were not available to help when needed. They were sitting on their cushions, separating themselves from others, thinking they were special, most likely developing arrogance. That is not the practice of Zen.

The practice of Zen is seeing arrogance for what it is—the greatest affliction and obstacle to peace. Whatever causes arrogance to develop must be cut off at the pass. A great danger in all practices is the development of this arrogance, righteousness, or false pride. We can easily feel we have all the right answers, the special practice, the holy way to the truth. Zen eschews all such reactions. The true hero of Zen is the doorman who is simply there to help.

> He affected everything not by domination, but just by being true.
>
> —*the Buddha*

Bowing to Everything

Once a person becomes a doorman, he or she is able to bow to everything. For some in the West bowing presents difficulty, as they may recall injunctions against idol worship in their own religious practices. To bow in front of a statue may be forbidden to them. It is important to discuss this crucial matter and to come to terms with it in the West.

First, to many Zen is not a religion, but a practice of purification and enlightenment that can be applied to all religious observances. It can be applied to martial arts, flower arranging, daily life, prayer, and any other activity the individual engages in. Zen allows us to taste the activity directly, not through layers of thoughts and ideas. If the practice of bowing is not acceptable to an individual, he or she simply need not physically bow. But one must bow within oneself, surrender ego, and give reverence to all of life.

From the Zen point of view, bowing represents a relinquishing of ego and delusion, and accepting the enlightened mind. It is a surrender of the small self to the good of all. It is an acknowledgment of the other, and the value and worth of the universe we are in. We can bow to others in many ways, not just physically, and indeed must do so. It is important to take the attitude behind bowing to every person we meet along our way.

This bowing is a stopping and an acknowledgment of the value and beauty of what is before you. It is a wonderful way to break out of our false ego and pride. It is a recognition that we are not the center of the entire world, but are willing to respect, honor and serve it. As Suzuki-roshi said:

> Bowing is a very serious practice. You should be prepared to bow, even in your last moment. Even though it is impossible to get rid of our self-centered desires, we have to do it. Our true nature wants us to.
> —*Suzuki-roshi*, Zen Mind, Beginner's Mind

The true man of no rank is free to interact with all of the world. He or she is the one bowing happily. He or she recognizes that our self-centered desires, encased delusions, pride, and arrogance have no reality.

Suzuki-roshi speaks of this in greater depth.

By bowing we are giving up ourselves. To give up ourselves means to give up our dualistic ideas. So there is no difference between zazen practice and bowing. Usually to bow means to pay our respects to something which is more worthy of respect than ourselves. But when you bow to Buddha, you should have no idea of Buddha, you just become one with Buddha. When you are one with Buddha, one with everything that exists, you find the true meaning of being.

Sometimes a man bows to a woman, sometimes a woman bows to a man. Sometimes the disciple bows to the master; sometimes the master bows to the disciple. Sometimes the master and disciple bow together. Sometimes we may bow to cats and dogs.

Bowing helps eliminate our self-centered ideas. This is not so easy. It is difficult to get rid of these ideas, and bowing is a very valuable practice. The result is not the point; it is the effort to improve ourselves that is valuable.

ZEN IN ACTION

Exercise 1: Bow to Everyone

Today, bow in your mind (or physically if you can or care to) to every person you have an interaction with. Before you start interacting with the person, take a moment and bow. See how this changes the quality of the interaction. See how it affects the quality of your day.

Exercise 2: Bow to Those You Have Difficulty With

Make a point of bowing (in your mind or physically) to three people you are having difficulty with. Keep doing it until the difficulty is gone.

Exercise 3: Bow Before Fighting

Just as a fight is about to begin between you and your partner, stop a moment and bow, either physically or in your mind. Then see how you feel. Bow to your desk before you sit down to work at it, bow to your food, to your friends, to your car. Bow to the morning; stop and bow to a sunset.

Exercise 4: Let the True Man (Woman) of No Rank Speak Out

Write a few pages about who you think you are. What are your strengths and weak points? How and who do you want to be?

Put this page aside. Open up a clean page and let the true man (or woman) of no rank speak and tell you what he or she thinks about that.

Exercise 5: Be a Doorman

How can you be a doorman today? Where are you needed? What will you do about it? When?

Nyogen Senzaki in *Buddhism and Zen* speaks beautifully of the doorman, the true Zen student.

> America has had Zen students in the past, has them in the present, and will have many of them in the future. They mingle easily with so-called worldlings. They play with children, respect kings and beggars, and handle gold and silver as pebbles and stones.
>
> When he realizes the truth, he has no delusion concerning his personal desires nor his self-limited ideas. He knows that there is no ego entity existing in him, and sees clearly the voidness of all form as merely shadow. If you live in this kind of Zen, you can leave hell in your dreams of yesterday, and make your own paradise wherever you stand.
>
> Those without realization, who cheat people with false knowledge, will create a hell during their own lives.

JUST BE YOUR ORDINARY SELF

RINZAI'S SHOUT

Followers of the Way, as I see it, nothing is complicated. Just be your ordinary selves; wear your robes, eat your food, and having nothing further to seek, pass your time peacefully. You have come here from everywhere, seeking Dharma, seeking deliverance. You want to escape the three worlds. Idiots, if you want to get out of the three worlds where can you go? Do you want to know the three worlds? They do not differ from the sensation of listening to me now! One of your passionate urges, however fleeting, is the world of desire. Momentary anger is the world of form and a second's foolishness is the formless world. These are the furniture of your own house!

Followers of the Way, find the One who is lively before your eyes, who perceives, weighs and measures the three worlds, and puts names to them.

—*Rinzai*, Rinzai Roku

CASE 31: (FROM *MUMONKAN*— TRANSLATED AS *THE GATELESS GATE*)

Koan: Joshu Investigates an Old Woman

A monk asked an old woman, "What is the way to Taisan?" The old woman said, "Go straight on." When the monk had proceeded a few steps, she said, "A good, respectable monk, but he, too, goes that way."

Afterwards someone told Joshu about this. Joshu said, "Wait a bit, I will go and investigate the old woman for you." The next day he went and asked the same question, and the old woman gave the same answer. On returning, Joshu said to his disciples, "I have investigated the old woman of Taisan for you."

MUMON'S COMMENT

"The old woman only knew how to sit still in her tent and plan the campaign; she did not know when she was shadowed by a spy.

Though old Joshu showed himself clever enough to take a camp and overwhelm a fortress, he displayed no trace of being a great commander. If we look at them, they both have their faults. But tell me, what did Joshu see in the old woman?"

MUMON'S VERSE

> The question was like the others,
> The answer was the same.
> Sand in the rice,
> Thorns in the mud.

Katsuki Sekida has the following to say about the former koan:

Many monks who rested at the tea booth asked this question of the old woman. They may have been simply asking the way to the mountain, but the old woman's answer izmplied something more.

Zen teachers use the words, "Go straight on," to their disciples, exhorting them to go directly forward with their practice of Zen. The old woman deplored the fact that despite the monks' apparent respectability and zeal, she found them in fact mediocre, willing to follow others shiftlessly.

When Joshu went to investigate the old woman he had something in mind. He could see through the old woman with half an eye. To understand Zen is one thing; to demonstrate it in actual life is another. Joshu is exhorting you to see her for yourself as well.

Everything has two phases. When one gains, one gains; when one loses, one loses. What do you see in this old woman? Was her action met with appreciation or thanklessness? Can you go straight on, following her advice? Can you tell the difference between the monks, Joshu, and the old woman? Be careful! Some unexpected thorns may be waiting for you.

CHAPTER 16

THE ZEN
FISHERMAN

ZEN MIRACLE 16
We return to the marketplace with open hands.

A monk spent years in a mountain monastery meditating. In the deep beauty and silence of nature he attained deep insight and peace. Then time came for him to leave the mountain and return to the marketplace. He soon found himself amid noise, distraction, squalor. He was jostled by a rude man in the street and anger flared up within him. What happened to his precious peace? This monk was not yet fully cooked. In the midst of the crowded marketplace one's true understanding is tested and grows.

A common misunderstanding of Zen practice is that one must leave the world to accomplish it. Nothing can be further from the truth. The world is with us wherever we go, and true Zen attainment is lived right in the marketplace. The messier life gets, the better. The more life challenges and accosts, the stronger practice must grow. True equilibrium arises when one is constantly being thrown off their center. Unless one is tossed about, how can he find the still point within?

True equilibrium is vital and active, a living response to the movements of life. It is not a numb, dead, lifeless peace, which is counterfeit Zen—a withdrawal from the raw beauty of change.

A Grandmother at the Side of the Road

A grandmother who was very accomplished in her Zen practice was found one day sitting at the edge of the road sobbing loudly. One of her grandchildren had died and her wails reached near and far. Some Zen monks approached her on the road, saw and recognized her, as her reputation in wisdom had spread far and wide. They stared at her in amazement.

"You have practiced Zen for many years," they said. "How can you cry like this because your grandchild has died?"

She looked up at them scornfully. "How can I not?" she replied.

As we grow in understanding and our compassion develops, our ability to feel and express what is true develops as well. We become more human, not less. Unless our enlightenment is taken back to the roadside, into the marketplace, with hands spread out to help all other beings, it is not true practice, but a facsimile.

The Zen Fisherman

A practitioner who has returned to the market place can be called the Zen Fisherman. His/her practice has become ripe. He returns without pretensions and ego, without greed, anger, fear, or harmfulness. He does not return with special clothing and language, but naturally, just like everyone else. The stink of Zen is gone from him. He has no need to be or do anything special. Every day as it is, is special enough for him. He cannot be differentiated from anyone else milling about, and does not separate himself from others due to class, race, religion, or anything else. The Zen Fisherman has gone out to join the throngs. If you look for him, you cannot find him. He looks like any other fisherman sitting on the dock, waiting for a fish. Only the Zen Fisherman is not waiting for fish. He is not waiting for anything. He is just sitting there with the entire world. If something jumps into his net, he greets it and puts it back where it belongs. He has become the true man of no rank.

Unlike other religious crusaders or teachers, the Zen Fisherman has nothing to sell, no deals to offer, no wisdom to hawk. He arrives in the marketplace with empty hands. Some might call this unconditional love. In Zen it is not called anything. Words, fantasies, ideals, and descriptions have disappeared by now. There is just the pure experience of being available—to all of life—all the time.

Usually we think of the marketplace as a place separate from home. We go there to make deals, buy, sell, be part of the crowd. It is busy, active, filled with bustle. Some people there are rich, others are poor. Some get good buys, others get conned. There are clever, crafty men, and there are the fools. No one wants to be a fool. Everyone wants to come home with something valuable. Everyone wants a good deal.

The Zen Fisherman is completely happy to be a fool. Some call him the idiot. Whatever is offered, he takes it. He always gives the best back in return. He keeps no score and is happy with whatever turns up that day. He accumulates nothing, and is willing to take what is left over. People laugh at him behind his back. It makes no difference to him. He joins in the laughter. He wants to see others happy and well. He has not come to the marketplace to create a stir, to be in charge, or to teach anybody anything. Who he is, not what he says, is the unspoken teaching that is given by itself.

Normally when we go into the marketplace—whether it is the marketplace for business, relationships, love, knowledge—we go wanting to know what we are going to "get." We have our goods we are selling, whether it is our products, body, charm, wisdom, money. We want to get a good return. If we do, we are satisfied and feel smart and successful. If we get short-changed we feel like failures and wonder what our life is for. We are caught in the whirl of the marketplace, which actually takes, not gives, our treasure to us.

The Zen Fisherman realizes that the marketplace is wherever he is. It is never separate from him. He is never separate from it. The epitome of Zen practice is to blend into the marketplace with empty hands, to offer what is needed, and then to move on. There is no need for awards, applause, or recognition, because the Zen Fisherman recognizes himself. He sees himself in everyone he encounters and needs nothing more than that.

Is That So?

Hakuin Zenji was a highly esteemed monk. All in the town greatly respected his strong practice and disciplined life. One day a young woman in the town became pregnant. She was ashamed and frightened and told everyone that Hakuin was the father of the child. The entire town turned against him.

Hakuin heard of this. "Is that so?" he said.

Finally the child was born. The young woman gave the child to Hakuin.

Hakuin took the baby and cared for him dearly, like a grandmother. The townspeople thought the worst of him, and spoke ill of him everyday.

"Is that so?" Hakuin said.

Several years later, the true father of the baby returned to town and to the mother. They were both older now and ready to marry. They wanted the baby back. The couple went to Hakuin and told him their wishes.

"Is that so?" he said, and lovingly returned the child.

Now the townspeople heard the true story. They all gathered around Hakuin's little hut and showered him with praises day after day. Hakuin listened quietly.

"Is that so?" he said.

"*Is that so?*" is a koan. Whatever happened to him, good and bad, beautiful and ugly, harsh and kind, the great Hakuin replied, "Is that so?" These few words strike the pain out of our lives. They strike out delusion, fear, and heartlessness. They grab us deeply and return us to the heart of the matter.

Gain and Loss

This is the life of the marketplace. Gain, loss, fame, shame alternate as the high and low tides of the sea. The ripe Zen monk Hakuin was at ease with all tides, with all conditions that came to him. He was not hurt by blame nor made proud by praise, because he deeply saw the true nature of both of them. He lived in the marketplace as a source of blessings, but did not gather his strength from its ways and means.

This situation is beautifully expressed by Sosan in *On Believing In Mind*:

> The ignorant cherish the idea of rest and unrest
> The enlightened have no likes and dislikes:
> All forms of dualism
> Are contrived by the ignorant themselves.
> They are like unto visions and flowers in the air:
> Why should we trouble ourselves to take hold of them?
> Gain and loss, right and wrong—
> Away with them once and for all!

The entire force of Zen practice is to have us be in the marketplace of life with true understanding both of the marketplace and of ourselves. When all our roles, masks, and costumes are removed, when we see the fleeting or empty nature of all people and events, the marketplace becomes holy ground that we are privileged to walk on. This is the fruit of Zen practice. This is the direction it takes us in.

THE MARKETPLACE AND TEMPLE BECOME ONE

A Zen student, Jeff, went to a church during a religious holiday where there were intense prayer and very strong practice. At one point in the service the priest announced that talking was not permitted until that section had been completed; they were all approaching the most holy point in the services. The church grew silent as all prepared for the peak moments. Then, suddenly a fight broke out between two congregants. One started shouting at the other. The second man hit the other's prayer book. Everyone in the temple gasped. The first man started waving his arms and cursing his adversary. Nothing could be done to stop them. The priest banged on the podium for silence. The fighting continued. Everyone was completely shocked. The head of the church went over and said to the man, "You have to leave. You are disturbing the entire congregation. The forces of evil are at work here." The man cursed more loudly.

Finally, the Zen student, Jeff, walked over to the man with a playful smile on his face. He wasn't angry with this man, didn't think of him as dark or evil.

He said, "You know I'm one of the detectives outside taking care of the church."

The man stopped, "You are?"

Jeff chuckled, "Yeah, we thought the danger would be coming from outside, not inside tonight."

The guy smiled.

"Why don't we go outside together, take a walk and talk this over?" Jeff said. As Jeff put his arm around him, the man started to cry. At that moment Jeff was the Zen Fisherman. As the two of them walked out the door, it was time to get back to the prayers.

Prayers are needed, but so is flexibility. When something flares up, when acute pain and suffering arises, we need something more than powerful structure—we need the flexible heart of the Zen Fisherman.

The Great Need Before Our Eyes

We sit so we can feel and be with the great need before our eyes, and be with the great need that's in ourselves, too. That man who was crying is also us. We are also the Zen Fisherman, who winds his way, unnoticed, in marketplaces of all kinds.

A Zen student, Rebecca, was sleeping alone in a large home she was about to move away from. Very early in the morning, just as the light was beginning to dawn, she heard a loud banging on her front door. Startled, she bolted up in bed.

"Who is it?" she called at the top of her lungs.

"It's me, Mike," a voice called back.

Frantic, Rebecca tried to think who this could be.

"Open up. Let me in. I rode my bike for an hour to get here."

"I don't know who you are," Rebecca called.

"You've got to remember me," the pained voice called back. "I slept over here lots of nights. I'm Josh's friend."

Suddenly Rebecca remembered that one of her sons had a friend who had recently gone mad.

"It's too early in the morning, Mike," she called back.

"Let me in."

"It's too early."

"Are you telling me I'm all alone?" he cried.

Frozen with fear Rebecca called back, "No, I'm telling you, I'm all alone here."

He seemed to like that better. The banging decreased.

"Well, then, come over to my house," he called back. "I want to talk to you, to tell you things."

Rebecca wondered if she should call for the police.

"I want you to help me. Will you come right away?" Mike said.

"I don't know if I can," she called back.

"You mean you're abandoning me?"

What help can I give? she wondered.

Rebecca was not ripe. She was not ready. She was not a true Zen Fisherman. A Zen Fisherman would have immediately opened the door, and welcomed the caller. Rebecca was still living in fear.

Galen tells the story that a great physician asked one of his assistants to give him a certain medicine.

"Master, that medicine is for crazy people," the assistant said. "You're far from needing that."

Galen replied, "Yesterday a madman turned and smiled at me, did his eyebrows up and down, and touched my sleeve. He wouldn't have done that if he hadn't recognized in me someone congenial."

If Rebecca had seen that which was congenial between her and Mike things could have been different. If she had seen how we are all madmen, then there could have been nothing to fear. Anyone that feels drawn, for however short a time, to anyone else, those two share a common consciousness. As Vimilakirti, a great Zen teacher, said, "I am sick because all beings are sick."

Had Rebecca been able to exchange herself for another, healing could have happened for both of them.

Psychologically speaking, there may be other responses and interpretations of this situation. Some may ask about skillful means. Was there true physical danger to Rebecca? Wasn't it appropriate to create proper boundaries and circumstances in which to help Mike? From a psychological point of view, of course, we answer these points positively. From the point of view of the Zen Fisherman, healing takes place differently. Some may ask if there isn't a danger to leave one's door open to all that come to it. The Zen Fisherman will respond by pointing to the much greater danger of living behind locked doors, danger to Mike and also to Rebecca. This poem by Rumi provides wonderful instruction for both of them.

Cry Out in Your Weakness

Take the cotton out of your fears, the cotton of consolations,
so you can hear the sphere-music,
Push the hair out of your eyes.
Blow the phlegm from your nose,
and from your brain.
Let the wind breeze through.
Leave no residue in yourself
From that bilious fever.
Take the binding from around your foot
Loosen the knot of greed
Give your weakness to the One who helps,
And let the milk of loving flow into you.
Be patient. Respond to every call that excites your spirit.
Ignore those that make you fearful and sad, that
Degrade you back to disease and death.

The Zen Fisherman appears in all traditions. He has transcended smallness and fear. In the ten ox-herding pictures in *The
Three Pillars of Zen*, the Zen Fisherman is beautifully described.

> The gate of his cottage is closed and even the wisest cannot
> find him. His mental panorama has finally disappeared. He
> goes his own way, making no attempt to follow the steps of ear-
> lier sages. Carrying a gourd, he strolls into the market; leaning
> on his staff, he returns home. He leads innkeepers and fish-
> mongers in the Way.

> Barechested, barefooted, he comes into the marketplace.
> Muddied and dust-covered, how broadly he grins!
> Without recourse to mystic powers,
> Withered trees he swiftly brings to bloom.
>   —The Three Pillars of Zen

ZEN IN ACTION

Exercise 1: Where Is the Marketplace?

Take note: Where is the marketplace of your life? Where do you
buy and sell your wares? What kind of returns are you hoping
for? Have you ever received them? Did they bring you what you
were looking for?

Exercise 2: Is That So?

Whatever happens to you today, tomorrow, and the next day,
respond by saying, "Is that so?" Continue this. Look at the world,
at yourself, and at your life out of the eyes of this powerful koan.
Go into it deeply, morning and night. Let it permeate each breath
you take. You think it's hard to do it? Is that so?

Actually, it is much harder to live in the marketplace of life,
buffeted about, without this koan. When the thrills and chills of
winning and losing subside, when the noise of the circus dies

down, and the roar of the rides at the amusement park dim, when you are left alone looking up at the dark nighttime sky, you will be grateful to have dwelt with it.

Is that so, done relentlessly, brings silence, peace, and true understanding. Without this we live a life caught up in masks and games. Nothing wrong with the masks and games, as long as we know that we are dressed up in them, and they do not replace our true skin and bones.

CASE 36: (FROM *MUMONKAN*— TRANSLATED AS *THE GATELESS GATE*)

Koan: *When You Meet a Man of the Way*

Goso said, "When you meet a man of the Way on the path, do not meet him with words of silence. Tell me, how will you meet him?"

MUMON'S COMMENT
"In such a case, if you can manage an intimate meeting with him it will certainly be gratifying. But if you cannot, you must be watchful in every way."

MUMON'S VERSE
Meeting a man of the Way on the road
Meet him with neither words nor silence.
A punch on the jaw:
Understand, if you can directly understand.

PART FIVE

Zen, God, and Enlightenment

CHAPTER 17

Walking Through the Gateless Gate

ZEN MIRACLE 17
The gateless gate opens. We walk through.

The ways you think you are, not the ways you really are, are the bars on your personal prison.

—Modern Zen teaching

The longing for freedom, for love, God, enlightenment is deep within all of us. We call it by different names and experience it in various ways—some as a search for truth, others as grace—or the yearning for the beloved—some as the removal of constriction from their lives, or the accomplishment of a life mission. In Zen we experience it as waking up from a deep, relentless dream.

Although many things in our temporary world seem to cause us pain, it can be said that the primal longing for enlightenment, or God, when unfulfilled, is the cause of all our suffering. Once this longing has been met, everything else in the world simply comes and goes, and we can receive it as part of the dance of the universe. In the Hindu tradition this is called *leila*, play, and the awakened ones are described as playful, filled with joy and song.

For them events are enjoyed as part of the intricate tapestry of life.

> An enlightened person is a continuous laughter.
> He is not a serious man, as ordinarily thought.
> Whenever you see seriousness,
> Know well something is wrong—
> Because seriousness is part of a diseased being.
> No flower is serious unless it is ill.
> No bird is serious unless it is ill.
> An awakened man realizes life is a song.
>
> —*Baghwan Rajneesh*

However, when our primal longing is not fulfilled, whatever we achieve, or receive can never bring peace and satisfaction. As a result most lives are beset by obstacles, hindrances, and limitations. Most experience themselves as prisoners of their jobs, environments, families, relationships, illnesses, or other circumstances. These difficulties and limitations can be seen as gates we are up against, which lock us inside, preventing us from moving freely through life. Each koan we receive in Zen practice is also a gate. As we solve each koan, the key keeps turning so that suddenly the entire gate opens and we can walk through.

The Gateless Gate

> Once you pass through this gate you can walk freely through the universe.
>
> —*The Three Pillars of Zen*

Our entire lives are built upon the idea of limitation and struggle. The yearning for freedom, the yearning to transcend the experience of limitation asserts itself constantly, both in our work on koans and in our experience of life. As we continue to practice we realize that the experience of limitation arises from the sense of a separate, unreal self, struggling to assert its reality and survive in an environment that seems to be hostile to its needs.

The peak moments of an individual's life are those in which this separate sense of self vanishes, along with all its ingrained desires. These primal experiences can be experienced in various ways, during prayer, lovemaking, meditation, music, art—whenever separation from life dissolves and the person returns to his original home. This original home can also be called Source, God, the Beloved, or Universal Wisdom.

Many seek this experience by taking drugs, alcohol, or other substances that momentarily lift the bonds they feel chained in. For those brief moments they walk through the gateless gate and taste their original nature. But depending upon how they arrive there, depending upon how they integrate the experience, the return back to "everyday reality" can take a toll. We know their experience of oneness is valid if after the return the person is more than he was before he left. His being has altered. He stands rooted in a deeper place.

If, on the other hand, he is wiped out, hung over, subject to distortions, hallucinations, bursts of rage, or otherwise impaired in his functioning, we know that the experience was induced by counterfeit substances, and that now he must pay the price. In all aspects of life there are counterfeits and shadows that produce reverse effects. Great care and patience are needed. Walking through the gateless gate requires wisdom, grace, and preparation. It cannot be grabbed at cheaply. It is not a quick way out of troubles or a free lunch.

The Way Out

The way out is simple and readily presented to us. The whole world presents it to us. We imagine we are locked and trapped inside a room, or a life, with no escape. But there is a door right in front of our eyes. Rather than open it and walk through bravely, we scramble around climbing the walls, dangling from windows, or pacing madly in the room, repeating the same patterns end-lessly. Then we run to all kinds of doctors, who are unfortunately locked there inside with us.

In a sense we are all like madmen, locked up, and suffering greatly, but refusing to simply walk through the door. *A solution like that is too obvious*, we think, *it's for children*. The idea that there's always been a door there waiting could even make us look like fools, and the greatest terror for those locked in the room, is to look foolish. They all want to seem smart. Some view them-selves as successful, significant, and powerful people. Others feel that life in the room, without them, could not go on.

When they look at the door in the middle of the room, oth-ers refuse to believe it's a door. They think someone must be trick-ing them. They're too smart to fall for something so basic. Some fall in love with their trap. They become addicted to running around helplessly complaining to anyone who will listen. Others love to run fast around the edges. The faster they run, the more powerful they feel. In their despair of ever getting out, many for-get that they are prisoners, and that there's a shimmering world waiting outside.

Walk Through

According to Zen the way out is easy. Just go to the door, turn the doorknob, and walk through. The way out is right in front of your eyes. It is everyone's birthright to walk through the door and be able to see vast sky outside. Nothing is hidden. All is revealed. Searching far is not necessary. Look—the door is right there.

A married couple came to see a Zen Master. The wife was pregnant with their fifth child. The husband was ill at ease and despondent, feeling he could not care for so many children.

The Zen Master offered them tea, and they all sat quietly drinking the green tea together.

"How can I have another child?" the husband finally asked fretfully. "As it is, I feel drained and overextended. I have nothing left to give."

The Zen Master drank his tea slowly.

The desperate husband looked at him. "There's a limit to how much pressure you can put on a person. Please, tell me, what more can I give?

"Maybe all the child needs," replied the Zen Master, "is the chance to open his eyes and look at the sky."

How many of us really open our eyes and look at the sky? How many care to? How many think all the treasures they can find are hidden inside the tiny room they're locked in?

In order to find the door and open it up, several things are necessary. These are ingredients of the medicine we are taking. These ingredients are both the fruits of practice and aids along the way.

Know That the Door Is There

First, we have to *know that the door is there*. This can also be called *faith*. In this practice it's a basic assumption we proceed from, and eventually becomes personal knowledge that grows as we sit. Whether we can presently see it, there is a door in front of our eyes. Because we are so blind, it can be hard to see it, but the door is always there. The way out of our personal prison is not more than a breath away. At any moment we can find it. And, even if we find it and then lose it, it has never gone anywhere. It's always waiting for us to return to it. No one is excluded.

The practice of zazen when done calmly, clearly, and continuously clears away enough of the fog so we can see the door. It builds our lives and awareness soundly. As Suzuki-roshi says,

If you continue this simple practice every day you will obtain a wonderful power. Before you attain it, it is something wonderful, but after you obtain it, it is nothing special. It is just you yourself, nothing special. As a Chinese poem says, I went and I returned. It was nothing special. Rozan famous for its misty mountains; Sekko for its water. It is a kind of mystery that for people who have no experience of enlightenment, enlightenment is something wonderful. But if they attain it, is nothing. But yet, it is not nothing. Do you understand? For a mother with children, having children is nothing special. That is zazen. So, if you continue this practice, more and more you will acquire something—nothing special, but nevertheless something.

—Zen Mind, Beginner's Mind

Two Men on a Train

One night a student went to the zendo and sat down next to an old Zen friend, for whom she particularly cared. What does it mean to sit with an old friend? It doesn't mean to gossip or chat, but to just sit still in the silence beside one another, breathing. As she sat, she was reminded of a story by Martin Buber.

One cold, winter evening two men boarded a train and sat down next to one another. One man opened his paper to read it during the ride and the other occupied himself with papers from the office. The two men were complete strangers, unknown to one another. As the train drove to its destination, both men remained occupied with their tasks. Then, suddenly, out of nowhere, a veil between them lifted. Though neither looked at one another or said a word, communication streamed back and forth between them. They were gripped. Each had a total sense of knowing one another, everything about the person, the so-called stranger on the train. Buber said, "It spoke, and the two men sat there and allowed it." Then, at the next station, one of the men got up and walked out of the train. The other felt complete, as if he had a "true meeting, really knew the man on the seat besides him." His sense of separation and isolation vanished.

This is an exquisite description of walking through the gateless gate. Where were the locks on this gate before? How did they open? At the moment the veils lifted the two men were not doing zazen—zazen was doing them. Neither had to know details about the other's life, his age, job, financial situation, or life history. In fact, all those ways we usually know one another keep the gateless gate closed tight. Our social contact with others focuses upon those kinds of details, but what happened on the train returns us to the essential truth. This kind of "meeting," or communion, doesn't have to happen only with a person, it can happen with a flower, tree, animal. Zazen practice prepares us for this lifting of the veil. When we are gifted with these moments of communion, we are never the same again.

Dogen Zenji says:

> To study Zen is to study the self. To study the self is to forget the self.
>
> To forget the self is to become one with all things.

On the train those two men suddenly forgot the self. They forgot their small self-centered concerns and opened to the wholeness. Actually, they were already united. It was only their obsessive involvement with their small selves that kept them from realizing this before.

NOTHING SPECIAL

It is very important to emphasize this *nothing special* aspect of enlightenment. By doing so we remain firmly planted in our lives in the everyday world, and also avoid the pride and arrogance that can accompany such an experience and cause more separation, taking us right back where we started from.

Nothing special means that enlightenment itself is natural, intrinsic, and should be taken as such. It actually happens to us many times during our lifetime, is part of the ongoing flow of growing up. When we look for it in places that are too out of the ordinary, we might end up with the opposite.

As a person practices awareness, or zazen, he returns to his original home. This happens every time he sits on the cushion, though he may not realize it. For some, enlightenment, or *kensho* as it is called, is an intense experience. There is a sudden, dramatic loss of limitation, or experience of piercing insight. Bliss or great joy can accompany this. Tears can pour—life is seen differently. Old fears and obstacles can vanish. The gateless gate itself is seen to be unreal.

After walking through the gateless gate the person must return to the matters of everyday life before him. Certain obstacles or problems are gone forever, others are not. They may be much less solid, however, and seem easier to live with. Unless plain, daily practice is continued, all of this can fade into the background and become a dream. Unless this experience is well integrated with all aspects of daily life, it can become something extra, not something useful and relevant.

There are all kinds of reasons we come to Zen practice. When some come, they have a powerful illusion in the beginning that they will become enlightened and never suffer again. In a sense it is true, but not in the way they expect it. As the gateless gate opens, one becomes larger than suffering, holds it differently, can even welcome it sometimes.

False Images of Enlightenment

But one of the great obstacles to practice are the illusions we have of enlightenment and the disappointment that can follow. In a Sutra it speaks of someone who cut off his arms and legs in order to be worthy of enlightenment. We can develop incredible images and fantasies about how to become enlightened and what the effects will be. This is a great danger.

A student chanted for hours every day, transcended the world, and remained in bliss. He came to visit someone else in the group who had a heavy jug of water that she could not lift by herself. She asked him to lift the water and help her put it where it belonged.

He sighed, leaned over, picked up this heavy jug of water half-heartedly and it tipped and fell all over him. No one got to drink the water. That's the danger of being in too much bliss.

Zen practice is not about becoming a great saint or sage, some enlightened being who never again feels any pain. It is about slowly dismantling the dualistic mind that harms others and one-self and keeps the gateless gate of our lives shut tight.

Our dualistic mind tells us that there is a subject here and an object there, that we have to get something from others or put up walls to protect ourselves. As long as we have this orientation, suffering is inevitable. But those moments when we look at another and see our own selves, the gateless gate opens and suffering vanishes.

An Autumn Evening

A Zen student, Richard, was in his parents' home and sat down on a fence in the backyard one autumn evening, when suddenly all sense of separation between himself and the whole world was gone—Whoosh. He felt exquisitely at one with all beings and the loneliness he had carried with him for years vanished, like smoke. After that, of course, he wanted to hold on to this experience, to understand it. He left and went to a monastery for many years to practice Zen.

"And then my life was very hard," he said. You'd think after such a beautiful experience life would be beautiful, perfect. But no, it can get harder, and the practice is there like a backbone, to deal with the hardness when it comes.

> If you want to see if it's pure gold, you must see it through the fire.
>
> —*Ancient Zen saying*

There was fire in Richard's life, lots of difficulty. Finally he had to leave the monastery and return back to his everyday life with all its complications. Then he said, "Now I'm sitting on top of a hundred-foot pole." That means, "I'm stuck at a certain place in my life and I can't go further. I can neither get off the pole, nor stay on it. I'm just sitting there." Although he longed to return to the monastery for practice, circumstances prevented it. Living his everyday life and longing to be somewhere else continued for almost ten years. His "enlightenment" experience cut him in two.

This is also a famous koan students practice with. *Step off the top of a hundred-foot pole.*

Richard felt stuck on the pole because he held on to the idea that to do real practice only meant to go back to the monastery. But what was he doing every day from the moment he woke up? Nothing but practice, practice. No special practice, the hardest of all to do.

These are the two faces of Zen practice—sitting, and then stepping back into our lives and reacting differently to what we find there. If we simply stay in bliss all day, what happens when someone needs a hand?

> Riding this wooden upside-down horse,
> I'm about to gallop through the void.
> Would you seek to trace me?
> Ha! Try catching the tempest in a net.
> —*Gido*, Inscription over his door

ZEN SICKNESS

The experience of this much freedom can have different consequences. For some it becomes an addiction. Ordinary life seems meaningless and they spend their time chasing after enlightenment, or bliss. All they want is the freedom, oneness, or peace. This is called *Zen sickness*, or stinking of Zen. It happens to those who are in early stages of practice. Just because one has an enlightenment experience does not mean that the person is far along. It simply means that he or she has seen a crack in the gateless gate. If anything, now he or she needs to practice more.

We do not know what real practice is until we have been sitting for many years. Each year along the way we think we finally
understand. But if our practice is strong and honest, by the next
year we realize, that's not it. There is no end to discovery.

Joshu, the great Zen Master, had his first great enlightenment
at the age of sixty. He then stayed in the monastery and practiced
until he was eighty, so his enlightenment could grow ripe. When
he was eighty he left and established his own school and taught
until he was one hundred and two, spreading his light far and
wide. Many, many students were enlightened under him.

Another form of Zen sickness is a person believing, because
of some enlightenment experience, that he is special, better than
anyone else. He utters Zen phrases and looks at others with a
strange glint in his eyes. This kind of sickness needs treatment
immediately.

A famous Zen teaching says, "If you see the Buddha, kill the
Buddha." This has been widely misunderstood. It simply addresses
this particular Zen sickness. It means, if you see someone acting
like a great, enlightened being, pay no attention to him. Look
within for the enlightened one. Do not venerate others and lose
yourself.

What Is Wrong with Your Own Head?

Killing the Buddha is knowing you have a head of your own, that
you breathe through your own nostrils, that your heart is beating. It is dismissing external phenomena and authority and going
deep within. This can also be understood as finding the spirit of
the living God within. In the Bible it tells us to find the spirit of
the living God. In Zen it says not to hang on to the dead words
of old masters, but speak and know the One who is living now
within. This is the process of becoming free of false authority,
not being deceived or trapped by others. So many are caught in
the limitation of venerating false authority, attributing to others all the power and beauty they have, disempowering them-

selves in the bargain. Zen is a radical cure for this. But don't be fooled. Don't be trapped. Remember to find the "true teacher" within.

Unconsciously, we give responsibility for our lives to those we consider authorities. We adulate them and project upon them all the qualities we idealize. In other traditions, this blind worship of the false God is called *idol worship*.

DON'T WORSHIP IDOLS

There is a strong injunction not to worship idols, or to make false Gods. In Zen we take this seriously. We do not worship form or phenomena—just take it as it comes and goes. We do not make any external manifestation into an idol, or project our ideals outside ourselves. We do not look outside for answers, but have radical faith in the living spirit within. We become silent in order to be directly in touch with the "spirit of the living God." This is living as the true man of no rank.

To illustrate this, there is a famous story about Enyadatta (an ancient Zen student). One morning she woke up and didn't know where her head was. She ran around blind with fear, thinking her head was on other people's shoulders. After days of this, of desperately searching everywhere, of crying and calling for help, many advisors and doctors arrived, but no one could help her. Finally, a Zen Master appeared and suggested she stop running around, sit down quietly, not move, breathe, focus her dispersed energies, and become one with her breath.

After a few days of this Enyadatta became ecstatic with joy and began running around the room she was in, crying, "My head, my head, it's on my own shoulders."

Enyadatta had an enlightenment. She walked through the gateless gate. There was no gate, there was no loss, her head was never anywhere else. It was always on her own shoulders—she only dreamt she had been beheaded, had no way to navigate in this world. Her delusion drove her crazy. Now she saw something simple, that originally she was complete and whole. Enyadatta saw her Buddha Nature—that nothing was ever wrong with her. From the very beginning she had all she needed to lead a complete and joyous life. Seeing her Buddha Nature, she was driven to great relief and joy.

> An eighth of a difference
> and heaven and earth are set apart.
> —*Sosan*, On Believing in Mind

Her great joy was delicious, but was also part of the Zen sickness. Why are we so ecstatic with joy when we discover our head is where it belongs, that we are originally complete and whole? What could have made us believe otherwise?

Our Head Is on Our Own Shoulders

Every time we sit down on the cushion to do zazen, whether we realize it consciously, we are living from and expressing this basic truth—that our head is on our own shoulders, that all we need is given to us from within. We are not being deceived by others. We are not placing unreal expectations upon other human beings. This is expressed in the very nature of what we are doing—taking radical responsibility for our own lives. As we do this we can also assume responsibility for the precious world we live in.

Fear of Moving On

Francine had a persistent fear of illness and death since she was little. As she grew older this fear intensified, so that every time she became ill, even with the most minor condition, her heart beat uncontrollably and images of death occupied her mind. This intensifying situation caused her life to become more and more constricted as she sought desperately to avoid any person or place with germs.

Finally, she sought therapy for her condition and spent considerably time analyzing psychological factors, dreams, and associations from her childhood onward. Though she gained temporary relief, eventually her fears returned, even more forcibly than they had been originally. Desperate about what to do now, Francine decided to try Zen practice.

In the beginning she sat on the cushion tentatively, constantly questioning the value of what she was doing. As her doubting mind began to quiet, she allowed herself to go into the silence more deeply. Day by day, she entered the silence and returned. One day at sesshin she allowed herself to dive deeply into the heart of what felt like the abyss surrounding her. To her amazement, she returned filled with light and joy.

"My fear of dying died that day," she said later. "In a sense I died on the cushion. In that moment I realized that all is well."

During zazen practice we enter the silence, return home regularly. And then we come back again. This journey, made over and over, familiarizes us with another landscape causing many to feel they will no longer be strangers when their time comes to leave this temporary world. When we realize our origin, not only death, but also our life, are no longer frightening. We then become free to live the life we have before us fully, no matter how brief or fragile it may be.

WHERE WE ARE GOING

Not only Zen practice, but all practice returns us to our original home, to our source, God, our self, our original nature. When we realize where we are from and where we are going, it becomes incredibly clear to us that this is not our permanent home. As we realize it our tenacious grasping to this world, and to those who occupy it, lessens, bringing ease. When asked who we are now, we might well agree with Bassho:

A traveler,
Know me thus,
This autumn evening.

Viewing ourselves as travelers may take a while. Although we see others pass away, we believe we will stay here forever and become deeply attached to experiences we meet along the way. As attachment increases, the gateless gate closes. As painful attachments lessen and we see how fragile and temporary our time here is, each day becomes more precious, and death and loss become less frightening—sad, maybe, but terrifying, no.

Though the effects of practice differ from person to person, they are not essentially so important. What is profoundly important is the experience of passing through the gateless gate. Even though we have to go through it hundreds of times, each time we do the gate becomes wider, simpler to open, and the vista expands, like a great flower blossoming.

The Udambara Flower Blossoms

The Udambara flower is a flower said to bloom once every three thousand years. To see a fully awakened person is so rare it is like seeing an Udambara flower. However, once you see this, the fragrance from the flower will stay with you forever. You will never forget it.

That is our direction—to approach the Udambara flower, so rare, fragrant and refreshing. In a monastery in Japan it says,

The Udambara flower, although fallen from the stem,
Is still fragrant.

We have two images presented—the Udambara flower fallen from a stem, and someone sitting on top of a hundred-foot pole. We are all fallen, all stuck on a pole, and at the same time we are Udambara flowers, with the capacity for enlightenment that cannot be extinguished. We must learn to hold all of this in the palm of our hands.

ZEN IN ACTION

Exercise 1: Examine the Gate

Where are the gates that are locked in your life? What keeps you from walking through them? Spend time answering this.

Exercise 2: Let Obstacles Vanish

Remember a time an obstacle or hindrance that seemed impenetrable vanished easily. Take note of all the times this has happened in your life.

Exercise 3: Walk Through a Gate

Find one situation in your life that is limiting. Walk right through it today. Don't think about how. Just do it now. Do this every day for the following week. See yourself simply walking through.

> Even when you are not trying to achieve something extraordinary, it will come to you all by itself.
>
> —*Rinzai Roku*

RINZAI'S SHOUT

> Followers of the Way, as I look at it we're no different from Buddha. In all our various activities each day, is there anything we lack? There is no safety in the threefold world; it is like a burning house. Do not linger. The deadly demon of impermanence will be on you in an instant, whether you're rich or poor, old, or young.
>
> If you want to be no different from Buddha and the patriarchs, then never look for something outside yourselves.
>
> Followers of the Way, this thing called mind has no fixed form; it penetrates all the ten directions. In the eye we call it sight, in the ear we call it hearing; in the nose it detects odors, in the mouth it speaks discourse; in the hand it grasps, in the

feet it runs along. Why do I tell you this? Because you seem to be incapable of stopping this mind that goes rushing around everywhere looking for something. You should stop and take a good look at yourselves.

—*Rinzai Roku*

CASE 16: (FROM *MUMONKAN*— TRANSLATED AS *THE GATELESS GATE*)

Koan: When the Bell Sounds

Ummon said, "The world is vast and wide. Why do you put on your robes at the sound of the bell?"

MUMON'S COMMENT

"In studying Zen, you should not be swayed by sounds and forms. Even though you attain insight when hearing a voice or seeing a form, this is simply the ordinary way of things. Don't you know that the real Zen student commands sounds, controls forms, is clearsighted at every event, and is free on every occasion?

"Granted you are free, just tell me: Does the sound come to the ear or does the ear go to the sound? If both sound and silence die away, at such a juncture how could you talk of Zen? While listening with your ear, you cannot tell. When hearing with your eye, you are truly intimate."

MUMON'S VERSE

With realization, things make one family;
Without realization, things are separated in a thousand ways.
Without realization, things make one family;
With realization, things are separated in a thousand ways.

CHAPTER 18

ZEN AND GOD

Walk wholeheartedly with me.
—*The Torah*

ZEN MIRACLE 18
We can love God with all of our heart,
our soul, and our might.

Many individuals question whether Zen is a religion. What is the relationship between zazen and God? Zazen in and of itself is neutral. It is a universal activity, inherent in all beings, like breathing, sitting, standing, walking. It is basic to all of us, something we all share. All beings love, hate, hope, fear, and need to be one with that which is greater than themselves.

In the Jewish scriptures it says that the sages of old would sit for one hour, pray for an hour, and then sit for another hour once again. They sat for an hour to prepare themselves for prayer, for the awesome task of facing their Maker. After prayer, they sat once again for another hour to absorb the effects and influences. Christians, Muslims, Hindus, and those of all different religious persuasions all have times and ways of entering the silence, being still, turning to that which is beyond their small minds.

PURIFICATION

Zazen itself can be viewed as a practice, not a religion. It focuses upon the individual, and the purification he and his life must undergo. It does not address the question of God, but keeps the focus, instead, upon the One who is turning himself or herself toward the infinite. When individuals are confused, anxious, or angry they may not be available to anything but the world of delusion they are caught in. Zazen is a practice of purification, making the person simple, clear, open, and available to the experience of the infinite, anyway he or she can receive and honor it.

The word *God*, and its many derivatives, can mean something different to each person. Wars have been fought in the name of God; people have been slaughtered, rejected, condemned. Lives have been cut short. One religious group often hates another, all in the name of the one God who creates and unites us all. Much confusion and misunderstanding have arisen out of this false understanding. In the Bible there is a strong injunction not to worship false Gods, not to worship idols, or our self-created, false understanding of God.

In Zen we do not describe God intellectually, but experience the great mystery in our flesh and bones. It can be said that in the practice of just sitting, as we return to our original nature, we are returning to the purity and essential goodness of God. As we become simple and harmless, we become fit vessels to express and live the many commandments and precepts we have been given— to make them real in our lives.

For instance, we read the injunction to love your neighbor as yourself. But how do we do this? Just saying these words again and again are not enough. How many can love their neighbors as themselves? So few even love themselves, or have had a taste of deep compassion. How many are open to truly being a neighbor, to befriending the stranger and welcoming them into their worlds? If in fact this precept were alive, we would have no homeless people on our streets.

It is said that Abraham was the greatest servant of God because his tent was always open to travelers, to strangers. He welcomed everyone in and gave them nourishment—material nourishment and spiritual nourishment. He taught them the true way of God. This is also the way of true Zen.

WHEN YOU COME WE WELCOME, WHEN YOU GO WE DO NOT PURSUE

When you come we welcome,
When you go we do not pursue.
—*Ancient Zen saying*

All are welcomed, regardless of race, religion, social status, life styles. All are given a place in the tent. When it is time for visitors to depart, they are not controlled, hounded, or filled with guilt about moving onward in their lives. They are thanked for the gift of their presence.

In order to make the precepts of all religions come alive, to manifest them daily in our lives, we must come face to face with that within ourselves which prevents it. We must become acquainted with our own selfishness, cruelty, greed and sorrow, so that they may become fully dissolved. It is crucial to have a practice of awareness and purification so that we do not lull ourselves into self-righteous dreams and believe we are following God's commandments, when in fact, our lives testify to the opposite, to prejudice, exclusion, hatred, and harm.

As we dissolve the poisons within ourselves, the presence of God becomes manifest in our tiniest dealings with one another, with our environment, and with all that is given us to do. We become more and more available to understand and respond to the great scriptures which point to the need for surrender to that which is larger than ourselves, to the spirit of the living God.

Some individuals who practice Zen are devoted Buddhists; others practice Judaism, Christianity, Hinduism, Islam. Some use their zazen to tend to gardens, cook nourishing food, care for their friends, or communities. Just as no two individuals have similar fingerprints, the way zazen manifests is unique for each person practicing. There are no injunctions or demands—instead, each is invited to find and sing the song that is within them. Some experience their own religions more keenly. Others find different ways to express their love of God or life.

Whether one uses the word God, soul, universal self, higher self, endless dimension, higher power, or universal life, it all points to the same experience. Zen asks that we put words aside, so that we can put aside confusion and dissension, taste *This* directly and then offer it to the whole world.

> Kabir says—student, tell me,
> Where is God?
> He is the breath inside the breath.
> —*Kabir*

ZEN CAUTIONS

These past hundred years of Zen practice have been years of pioneering in America, transplanting new seeds into a wild frontier. They have been years of joy, laughter, sorrow, discovery, confusion, beauty, growth, and pain. As in any new venture, along with times of victory, there have been times of error and loss. In taking stock of practice thus far, it is necessary to look with an honest eye, not glossing over the dangers of practice, or creating more illusions that will leave the individual more lost than before.

Above all, Zen is practical. It reminds us to continually be present to what is happening in front of our eyes. It warns us not to use the practice to disregard that which we do not like. Denial runs deep in the human being. To use practice in the service of denial is a great danger we are all faced with.

True practice honestly notices and acknowledges whatever is happening, and uses skillful means to deal with it. Blind obedience is always off the mark. A pivotal part of practice is cleaning house, daring to take a broom and sweep the dust out vigorously.

Above all, this practice is geared toward humility, toward the eradication of ego, arrogance, power over others, and control. It is dedicated to dispelling illusions and lies. Zen practice appears as an antidote to all the forms of bureaucracy and hypocrisy that erode the simple, truthful experience of the individual. When practiced truly, it returns human dignity, power, and independence to the one who is practicing.

This is a caution against authority worship, against giving up one's own clear mind and believing the truth exists in someone else. Although there are many great teachers of Zen, these teachers are human and subject to delusion. They do their best, and we do our best to keep our sight clear. We fall, they fall, and then we both get up. When someone is falling, let us not delude ourselves and say they are standing tall. Too much unchecked power for one person always turns to poison. In all Zen centers it is necessary to have an antidote to this possibility. We all have responsibility for not allowing this to take place.

It is good to remember the old Zen saying:

There is Zen, but there are no teachers of Zen.

This leads us to realize that our own practice is our teacher, all we are and need to know is contained deeply within. A teacher comes to guide, encourage, inspire, and warn. At times it is also necessary for us to guide, encourage, inspire, and warn our teachers and Zen friends. No human being is infallible. This is the greatest caution of Zen.

ZEN MIRACLE COMMANDMENTS

Here are some essential guidelines from the book. Keep them as a companion and enjoy living with them.

- Do not lean on others. Do not lean on anything.
- Keep your back straight at all times. Your spine connects heaven and earth. Honor it.
- Loneliness is an unwillingness to communicate freely with all of creation. Remedy this.
- Do not puff yourself up and put others down. We are all treading on the same earth.
- This particular breath will not come again. Pay attention to it.
- We cannot stop the noise, but we can stop ourselves. We can accept the noise.
- What you are at this moment contains the whole message of what you were.
- You can never see anything worse than yourself.
- Place after place is the right place.
- Don't put a head on your own head. What's wrong with your own?
- Going somewhere doesn't take you anywhere else.
- Doing nothing is more than enough. Flowers grow on their own.

BIBLIOGRAPHY

Beck, Charlotte Joko. *Everyday Zen*. New York: Harper and Row, 1989.

The Book of the Zen Grove. Livingstone Manor, N.Y.: Zen Studies Press, 1984.

Chodren, Pema. *Start Where You Are*. Boston: Shambhala, 1994.

The Diamond Sutra and The Sutra of Hui-Neng. Boston: Shambhala, 1990.

Dogen Zenji. *Shobogenzo*. Daihokkaikaku Publishing Co., 1975.

Endless Vow, The Zen Path of Soen Nakagawa. Boston: Shambhala, 1996.

Kapleau, Roshi Philip. *The Three Pillars of Zen*. New York: Anchor Books, 1980.

Mud and Water: A Collection of Talks by Bassui. San Francisco: North Point Press, 1989.

Senzaki, Nyogen. *Buddhism and Zen*. San Francisco: North Point Press, 1987.

Thich Nhat Hanh. *Being Peace*. Berkeley, Calif.: Parallax Press, 1987.

Uchiyama, Kosho. *Opening the Hand of Thought*. Arkana, 1993.

Two Zen Classics: Mumonkan, Hekignaroku. New York: Weatherhill, 1977.

Suzuki Roshi. *Zen Mind, Beginner's Mind*. New York: Weatherhill, 1989.

The Zen Teachings of Master Lin-Chi. Translated by Burton Watson. Boston: Shambhala, 1993.

INDEX